Divine Feminine Energy:

Goddess Spiritual Secret Energy. Manifesting for Women and Healing Your Soul Through Ancient Spirituality. Awakening Secrets you Never Knew About.

Contents

- **INTRODUCTION** 1
- **CHAPTER ONE** .... Error! Bookmark not defined.
- **WHAT IS FEMININE ENERGY?** 4
- **QUALITIES OF THE FEMININE ENERGY** 5
  - **Empathy** 5
  - **Vulnerability** 7
  - **Multitasking Focus** 10
- **HOW TO IDENTIFY YOUR FEMININE ENERGY** .. 10
- **HOW TO BRING OUT YOUR FEMININE ENERGY WITH EASE** 15
- **CHAPTER TWO** 17
  - **THE ESSENCE OF YOUR FEMININE ENERGY** 17
- **HOW TO UTILIZE YOUR FEMININE ENERGY** 20
- **THE NEGATIVE EFFECT OF THE FEMININE ENERGY** 24
- **SIGNS OF HIGH FEMININE ENERGY** 27
- **CHAPTER THREE** 29
  - **THINGS THAT DRAIN YOUR FEMININE ENERGY** 29
- **WAYS TO REFILL YOUR FEMININE ENERGY** 40
- **CHAPTER FOUR** 43
  - **THE WOMAN WHO LOVES HERSELF WHOLLY** .. 43
  - **How to Love Yourself and Influence Your Feminine Energy.** 52
- **CHAPTER FIVE** 56

FEAR AS AN HINDRANCE TO FEMININE ENERGY 56

SURROUND YOURSELF WITH PEOPLE THAT REFLECT WHO YOU WANT TO BE 57

THE WORLD IS YOURS FOR YOUR TAKING 58

BE PREPARED TO FAIL. 60

BE PREPARED TO SUCCEED 60

CHAPTER SIX 63

EMPOWERING YOURSELF AND BOOSTING YOUR ENERGY, AND MORPHING INTO YOUR BEST SELF 63

BOOSTING YOUR ENERGY 67

MORPHING INTO YOUR BEST SELF 72

How to be Your Best Self 73

How to Manage Your Time: 76

HOW TO TRANSFORM INTO YOUR BEST SELF ... 80

CHAPTER SEVEN 83

ENERGY VAMPIRES 83

TYPES OF ENERGY VAMPIRES 84

   The Gaslighting Vampire 84

   The Clueless Vampire

   The Narcissist Vampire 86

   The Control Vampire 86

HOW TO SPOT AN ENERGY VAMPIRE 87

HOW TO DEAL WITH ENERGY VAMPIRES 90

HOW TO MANAGE ENERGY VAMPIRES 93

HOW ENERGY VAMPIRES AFFECT YOUR FEMININE ENERGY 96

WHAT TO DO IF YOU ARE THE ENERGY VAMPIRE 99

CHAPTER EIGHT 102

SELF-AWARENESS 102

TYPES OF SELF-AWARENESS 103

Public/External Self-Awareness 103

Private/Internal Self-Awareness 104

BENEFITS OF SELF-AWARENESS 104

BARRIER TO SELF-AWARENESS 106

SIGNS OF LOW-SELF AWARENESS 108

HOW TO IMPROVE YOUR SELF-AWARENESS ... 110

HOW SELF-AWARENESS BOOSTS YOUR FEMININE ENERGY 112

CHAPTER NINE 115

MEDITATION 115

TYPES OF MEDITATION AND WAYS TO MEDITATE 115

BENEFITS OF MEDITATION 124

HOW MEDITATION INCREASES FEMININE ENERGY 126

CHAPTER TEN 130

BE THE ONE WHO LEAVES WHEN IT BECOMES TOXIC 130

WHAT IS A TOXIC RELATIONSHIP? 132

TYPES OF TOXIC RELATIONSHIPS 132

Toxic Relationship And Mental Health 138

Getting Over a Toxic Relationship 142

How Staying In Toxic Relationships Affects Your Feminine Energy 143

CHAPTER ELEVEN 145

How To Utilize The Best of Your Feminine Energy 145

How to be in Your Feminine Energy at Work 150

Impacts of Ignoring Your Feminine Energy at Work 152

Some Signs That Your Masculine Energy has Overridden Your Feminine Energy at work. 153

CHAPTER TWELVE 156

UNLEARNING THE MYTHS ABOUT FEMININITY 156

CHAPTER THIRTEEN 167

FEIGNING STRENGTH IN WEAKNESS 167

There is something called an Apprentice Mindset. 168

Benefits Of Listening and Asking Questions 172

Cultivating a Healthy Attitude 178

CHAPTER FOURTEEN Be The Woman Who Takes Charge 180

    Learn about Finances 181

    Debt Management 182

Take Charge in your Relationship 183

    Here are Ways You Can Take Charge of Your Relationship 183

- **Take Charge of Your Well-being/Health** 184
- **Taking Charge of your Future/Life** 187
  - **Here are five ways to take charge of your future and life:** 187
- **Taking Charge of Your Happiness** 188
  - **Ways You Can Take Charge of Your Happiness** 189
- **A Little Love Note for You** 192
- **Conclusion** 192

INTRODUCTION

I have asked myself countless times if staying put while my strengths waste away would be a fair thing to do to myself. The new version of me would certainly not be pleased if I had let that happen. And to me, being able to do what people think I cannot do is power. But in the real sense, I was trying to force myself into being more masculine when I was supposed to recognize and acknowledge my feminine strength.

I've been scared to sit back and let people, men especially, foot my bills because a woman should have her own money, handle her well-being, and go out there to smash her goals and build the life of her dreams.

It feels like being a woman automatically takes away my right to choose what I want for my life. So I keep moving in circles created by societal perceptions of what people should be. I've gotten angry over not-so-obvious ill treatments by people who think I should be under a man. 'Keep shut, have kids, and cook or clean.' Even in the workplace, they try to tone down my ambition.

If I were contesting for a position in society, some male leader would tell me that my place is in the kitchen, not the office. It could be so offsetting and make us women vow to hit as many goals as we can in the professional world.

But I discovered I had wrong thought patterns regarding feminine energy. I learned that we all have both masculine and feminine energy and that there was nothing terrible about being a carrier woman. I just needed to recognize and acknowledge my feminine power. My journey through discovering what feminine energy is has been an eye-opener for me. And I think every woman should seek to know hers and use them to her advantage.

As human beings, we all have our powers deep inside of us. We are a lot more powerful than we think we are. But this power lies dormant in us until we awaken it and begin to utilize it. If you believe in your inner strength and energy, it will manifest and work wonders for you. But if you do not believe in it, it will remain inactive. You know, what you have faith in comes alive in you and for you.

This book focuses on women's feminine energy and how they can utilize it to the fullest. There is so much that women do not know about their feminine energies. It takes significant self-awareness to tap into your feminine energy as a woman fully. I have written this book as a guide to help you understand it, unlearn the myths, and know everything you need to know.

This book is written from the heart. I poured so much of myself into it for you, which is why I urge you to read through every word and bear in mind that I am rooting for you with all that I am.

I hope you enjoy reading this book as much as I enjoyed writing it, and I hope you see the magic that is your feminine energy in a new and brighter light.

Happy reading, my dear black woman. Be empowered, go out there, and show the world all the excellence you are made of!

CHAPTER ONE

WHAT IS FEMININE ENERGY?

Feminine energy is an inherent nature that causes a woman to behave in a certain way naturally or to carry herself in such a manner that screams 'naturalness.' I had gotten my letter of request for my industrial training to a company in West Africa, with hopes that I would be accepted. When I got the opportunity, I started to think of ways to impress my boss with work, goals, and marketing strategies, hoping that it'll show him how much I was fit for a career. I had subjected myself to so much pressure that I failed to see what I had to offer. I was so engrossed in doing my best and pleasing my employee that I did not remember the excellent work I would contribute to the company.

Mind you, it is not terrible for me to desire to give my best. What is awful is I forget how great I was at what I did and lose myself to please. There is a great need for balance in things like this because it takes so little to lose oneself.

My boss loved my passion for hitting goals and being "masculine" in my work life. But he loved, more than anything else, the fact that I was a listener; I was positive-minded, open, willing to learn, and give my best. These qualities never came across as work, weakness, or too feminine, creating a relationship that others would struggle with for even ten years before accessing. Those were my feminine energies!

Feminine energy expresses itself from inside to outside. And to tap into that, I discovered I had to put my worry, pride, and ignorance away and master it.

Feminine energy is one of the most compassionate yet potent human powers. Whenever I think of feminine energy, I think of a mother's love. It's so fluid, pure, and joyful. Feminine energy comes off as a weakness to some people, but they fail to realize that it is human nature to be full of softness and compassion. But it is not very obvious because the roughness of the world makes us strong-hearted and brutal even when understanding resides in our core.

QUALITIES OF THE FEMININE ENERGY

There are many qualities that scream feminine energy with great ease. These qualities are usually soft and gentle, and they are quite easy to identify. In this section of this book, I'll hold you by the hand through words and take you through the qualities of the feminine energy. Now, come with me!

Empathy

Empathy resides in the core of human beings. It makes you feel other people's pain even when you are not directly affected. Empathy tugs at your heart and persuades you to offer a helping hand to people in need. One of the essential qualities we apply as humans makes us feel like we've got each other. Like we can brave the turbulent storms of this world together and win.

I have had to be the connection to all of my friends because I decided to be more empathetic. I have a friend who finds it challenging to communicate effectively. Effective communication is the pillar that holds every great friendship or relationship together.

When she went on to study medicine overseas, she barely answered my messages and that of our other friends. What made the friendship we shared even more sour was when she came back home but wouldn't meet with us or tell us why. That singular act of hers caused us to fall out of friendship; we all assumed that she didn't want anything to do with it anymore.

Two of our friends had decided to stop being friends with her, and I did too, but I kept wondering if she was okay. And how I would feel if my friend preferred to put their emotions first before creating reasons why I may have acted the way I did.

There were strong reasons why she couldn't meet with us. One day, I had to talk to her about how worried I was. On doing that, I learned she was sick, lost her phone, and had to travel out of state because she could not stand many people who knew her seeing her like that. She was going through a lot. I would have lost a friend simply by not putting myself in my shoes!

Empathy has built more relationships than solving problems because humans want to feel understood and considered. It is one of the most potent feminine energies I've discovered. It has helped me build and sustain valuable relationships.

Going back, yes, it is unfair that she treated us the way she did. But that wasn't enough reason for us to give up on everything we shared as friends. Sometimes, our friends act like they're ignoring us and having the best life. But it is not always so because things may not be what they seem. Our friends could be hanging on thing threads and fighting for their lives while we allow our hardened hearts and lack of empathy to rob us of the last moments we may ever have with them again.

Vulnerability

Everyone is afraid to speak up because the world has set ridiculous standards for us all. So whether I feel okay or not, I dare not behave like a weakling. But that would be disconnecting from my nature as a human right? We are human beings and not robots. We are women with a wide range of emotions, and it is perfectly okay for us to feel different emotions at different stages of our lives. Of course, the world will tell us how weak we are to own up to our feelings and be vulnerable. But that's the world's problem. I will not allow the world to take the joy of being a human being from me for anything.

In many African communities, men cannot show weakness, ask too much, or cry. Because if they do so, they would be called dependent weaklings or pimps. I've had to ask myself why anyone would think it is wrong to be human. We want to express our worries, pain, hopes, and fears deep inside our hearts. We want to be held and encouraged. We want to drop the "all perfect and strong" facade and get real. We wish to express our inner child.

At a point in my life, I began to feel less attracted to people who saw my weaknesses or had to stand in for me at my darkest moments. It felt like I was showing too much and that they were encouraging my fault. I was afraid of needing them too much. But as time went on, I discovered that we all need each other in one way or the other.

When I found whom I was sure I could be open to, I stopped crying silently—opening up since then has been an exciting journey because of the profound healing it brings. Opening up won't heal you at once, but it speeds up your healing process because you get to share the things that make you wet your pillow with tears at night with a person that comforts you and assures you of the light at the end of the tunnel.

Nurturing

It screams feminine energy in every way, from raising a child to growing flowers in a garden or teaching children in school. Nurturing has helped build strong emotional connections between the nurturer and the cultivated. I began to see nature for what it truly is when I learned nurturing.

I would look at the sky and begin to think about the amount of wonder the world holds in such a way that the person seated right next to me connects so profoundly. I appreciated life more and told myself that everything I touched could be better than I had met it. With that in mind, I worked on the value I wanted to give humanity.

Now I walk without fear. I know that no one can steal my true nature wherever I go, and I can be independent because I have identified my strengths. And for me, that's what makes anyone powerful.

Knowing you can go worldwide and still build what you have lost screams energy!

To nurture is to love deeply. Promoting has a way of making our souls come alive. That is why therapists sometimes recommend gardening to help us get through difficult times. It takes a great deal of patience and cares to nurture. When we encourage, we open up the softest parts of us, and our feminine energies bare themselves in simple yet powerful ways.

Multitasking Focus

It is the energy that many men do not possess. It always feels like hard work or an impossible mission. I have had to listen to a vital podcast while I cook and entertain visitors. I do not know how I do it, but that makes me feminine. Multitasking increases my productivity daily, and I achieve a lot more because I can multitask.

Multitasking is another powerful feminine energy that I love with the whole of my heart. It keeps your productivity level up and helps you achieve great results. Whenever I have to do so many things, I tap into this feminine energy of mine and execute flawlessly like the powerful black woman that I proudly am.

HOW TO IDENTIFY YOUR FEMININE ENERGY

Owing to the depth and diversity of feminine energy, it is not always easy to spot it oneself. That is why I took my time to carefully write this book section to guide you when you want to identify your feminine energy.

My feminine energy helps me connect to myself in natural ways. I have had to close my eyes for a second to imagine what my life would be like if I were just myself. What activities was I lagging in that I would have loved to do but not do?

I love to relax deeply. You know, sitting back and resting while the world goes on. One needs a focused mind to relax in a busy world. At the place of relaxation, you can discover some essential things about yourself.

For example, I do not bother about doing anything when I take time off to rest; I embrace peace instead and relax. I do not prove points to anyone. Ideas flow because I allow my mind to wander independently. The more natural I am in my actions, the better my energy. Most of my masterpieces came to me when I relaxed. Relaxation keeps you away from the drowning noise of the world. In silence, you make brilliant discoveries.

My feminine energy helped me connect to people on a different level.

When I started to look at myself inwardly, I discovered I possessed excellent observation skills. So amazing that it awed the people around me. It didn't happen overnight. It took me some little studying to know that I was observing the right things and when I began to put it into practice, it changed everything. I could see how the people around me needed me to see what they were seeing and tell them what I thought before they went for it. That was energy!

My feminine energy allowed me to express myself in better ways.

In my journey to discover my feminine energy, I found I had hidden talents yet to explore. I started to write stories in a way that attracted every reader. I learned how great a cook I am and how much of a listener and team player I am.

Sometimes we need to step back and watch out for what we would be if society's perceptions were not shoved down our throats. When I discovered that my writing solves problems and has even gone as far as attracting money, I wasn't pressured to be a career woman anymore because I am already one!

I did not have to sit on a chair with a laptop in front of me in a professional setting to call myself a working-class woman. I had work already. And when I put those skills into practice, I loved myself more.

My feminine energy tells me it's okay to feel loved too. I have been a sucker for independence all my life. When I let people do things for me, it feels like I'm sitting on their heads. Letting people do something for me or give to me had been so tiring that I'd fallen sick from just receiving them. But I had to ask myself why I felt like I was not deserving of love too.

If I've had to work hard to give to others, why shouldn't I be given?

Receiving has a way of putting our vulnerability at risk. At first, it was pretty risky seeing that an independent woman like me hated to be disrespected. Still, the more vulnerable I was, the more I realized that I could not do everything alone.

I had to let the people headed specifically in my direction with help, favor, and love me. It has helped me channel my energy toward other essential things.

I believe that if all women can keep their masculine energy aside just a little and try to see the powers in them, they would feel more alive.

My feminine energy loves to be rather than do.
I have learned that being yourself is the best way to feel energetic. In this world, being yourself attracts mockery

rather than encouragement. I got a call from my boss to come back to the office to work for him with a promise of reasonable payment.

My boss had been so nice to me while I worked for him. That's a quality you hardly see, especially in most black men, because they need to feel important. But I declined the offer, not because I didn't need the money, but because I wasn't myself. I felt limited when I had to depend on my feminine energy. I felt creatively hungry and deprived of expressing myself.

That was because, in the corporate world, you are not allowed to be yourself if you are not the boss. So I found myself at home doing the things that made me feel like myself, and I watched how it helped me grow faster than a primarily working class would.

Even women have masculine energy and may prefer to work for corporate organizations.

We would be better off doing what we connect to the most. I would love to be the mastermind behind a significant change in society. In the movie, 'the greatest showman,' Phineas helped many people, especially women become more confident in their unique selves. That enabled them to use their talents excellently, and that's what feminine energy should do. It should help a person to become.

WHEN TO TAP INTO YOUR FEMININE ENERGY

The point of being feminine doesn't mean that a woman has to drop everything masculine about her and be feminine. It goes way beyond that. Every human has two sides to them, connecting us in every area of our lives.

When a man sees a woman taking the lead in her career, he instinctively sees strength and security. That makes him want to be her friend or partner. That's good, but we shouldn't focus on that alone. We should also look at the strength the woman embodies. When I discovered my feminine energies and mastered them, I began to choose when to use my masculine or feminine energy.

Here's a straightforward way I found out what masculine energy is like; I discovered that I always wanted to solve the problems I saw around me. I wanted to take on a project and know that it is executed excellently, most times to impress my boss or to get acknowledged or recognized by society. I wanted to be called a leader in a world where women are barely seen as one.

But when I learned that it is okay to have both masculine and feminine energies, life became more interesting. I realized that it wasn't about being typically feminine. Still, it was about knowing how and when to be feminine. In a setting where I have to be sympathetic, I drop all my masculinity and let myself feel what the person next to me is feeling. I do not tell myself that life moves on as a man would say to himself. I let myself be feminine, cry with them, try to support them emotionally, and speak words of love and encouragement.

It has gotten people to open up to the extent to which opening up helps them heal.

My feminine energy screams intuition. I have to listen to my mind when I've had to make crucial decisions. I do not sit down and begin to think of saving 10,000 lives with my decision. Even though it'll affect people; instead, I close my eyes and ask myself what feels wrong or right about the decisions I'm about to take.

I tap into my feminine energy when I have to be there for a friend, when I have to let my creativity do the speaking, and when I have to be in control of my world. That's when I begin to feel like I'm living and not existing.

I discovered that I hated the office environment and was just there to get the approval of anyone who thought a woman should work hard and achieve that much. But I discovered that I had achieved so much by knowing my inner and natural feminine strengths and using them to my advantage.

HOW TO BRING OUT YOUR FEMININE ENERGY WITH EASE

Meditate: this is the part where I have to close my mind to all distractions and allow it to wander into the place it wants me to go. That way, I discovered what makes me happy, what makes me sad, what I would instead not do, and what I should be doing. It wasn't clear at first, but the more I practiced, the more I explored.

Dance: this may feel unnecessarily goofy, especially for women who take life too seriously, but I have never seen someone who dances sadly. There's an energy I feel when I dance. It's like I forget all my worries, deadlines, and plans to focus on making myself happy. This has proven to be one of the fastest ways to make myself happy. I saw that by making myself happy, I developed a resistance to external pressure. That's sure a good energy to keep.

Emote: I discovered that my ability to emote lies in my stories. When I put a story out there, my readers always come back with news of how they either cried, felt pity and pain, or anger because of a character or plot in my story. Another way to emote could be by singing.

Other ways could be painting, dancing, and acting. Whatever the case, emoting is very strong and can bring even the most muscular men to the ground. The most beautiful thing about it is that it doesn't affect the people around me. Instead, I emote alongside whomever I cause to emote because of my natural sympathetic self.
We women would do better if we identified and explored our feminine energy.

CHAPTER TWO

THE ESSENCE OF YOUR FEMININE ENERGY

The feminine energy has been recognized worldwide because of its uniqueness in families, spiritual gatherings, and projects.

Society believes that feminine energy is needed for intuition in decision-making, choosing spouses, buying houses, investing, etc.

Since feminine energy carries intuition, most people believe that a woman can help her husband make better decisions, choose better friends or work better. This has been proven right in most cases, even when many others see it as a myth.

In the corporate world, bosses believe that when a woman is involved in a business decision or executive, she attracts clients' favor. They think she applies her intuition in planning a sound business strategy. While most business leaders depend on rules and methods to make a business successful, others rely on a woman to help them make decisions.

A young lady saw an advertisement about an upcoming event that involved selling products to make money. It was a moment of joy for her because she badly wanted to meet an icon in the business industry. She volunteered to help a fellow woman like her sell her products to be in her circle. She sent a message to the woman, telling her how she would be happy to help. The woman was delighted. On that day, she collected each product from the woman and went into the crowd to advertise. There, she met a man who looked confused. When she walked up to him, he was startled and apologized immediately.

She looked at him intensely and asked if he was okay. He affirmed, but she was sure that something was not right. When he insisted, she started talking about how scared she had been to make decisions regarding her career. His eyes brightened, and he told her why he was sad in a matter of minutes. His boss was looking for the brightest idea to take his business to the next level, and he doubted his idea was good enough to do that for the company.

She asked to see the idea. Being a business person, she could see that his concept was creative but not good enough to achieve the desired results. She decided to help him come up with a better one. After over twenty minutes of deliberation, they devised a better idea. He thanked her and was eager to go, but he stopped and asked her about her products. She marketed it as taught by the woman she was helping, hoping he would at least buy one. But he followed her and bought everything, telling them to share it with everyone there.

This story explains the significant impact of feminine power and how its purpose cannot be overemphasized.

The sympathy, patience, attentiveness, and intuition of the young lady helped everyone in the situation. Guess what! They are happily married and have become good business partners. And when the man is asked how his business keeps growing, he points at his wife.

The feminine energy works both directly and indirectly.

The feminine energy has helped me in my faith. Faith is believed to be that path you choose, with a strong belief that it will help you succeed. Often, it's challenging to be in the midst of chaos. The faith journey is not easy; it's chaotic sometimes because you'll be dealing with concepts whose roots you do not fully understand.

Sometimes I pray silently and tell myself that whatever comes to my mind, I'll use it as an anchor for my decisions.

It's like the feminine energy has been put in us to guide us through difficult times. The woman is believed to be a weaker vessel because the man is a more practical decision-maker, endures more hardship, and exerts more physical strength. But I think that the most vital forces are more emotional and mysterious. And this is one of the reasons why feminine energy would continue to help both men and women.

A woman is a pillar for her world when earthquakes of uncertainty, lack, desperation, and confusion persist. As a woman, I have practiced entering into my feminine zone to tap from my energy to fight hard. Every woman has that in her, and she should be able to use it for the right reasons; to protect herself and the ones she loves and to help in every other aspect of her life.

The essence of my feminine energy, I have learned, is to serve myself and humanity. The feminine energy is also seen in a mother's ability to love her child unconditionally.

In her poem about a mother's love, Joanna Fuchs write about how a child asks their mother how she found the energy to love them the way she did. She fought, exercised patience, and stood by them in everything.

Like her, we all ask those questions because it seems impossible. But the truth is that feminine energy is powerful, magical, and able to withstand many things. The ability to tap into my feminine power is one of the first ways to see my world and affect it positively.

HOW TO UTILIZE YOUR FEMININE ENERGY

The first step to utilizing your feminine energy is to accept it. The typical ambitious woman today believes that if she exercises her feminine energy, she will be seen as weak. But we do not realize that masculine and feminine energy can be used in any situation that demands them.

A few years ago, a woman needed to go out for marketing to attract more clients. She knew that she would need to impress her boss, so she deliberately wore masculine energy to help her achieve desired results. She would set her goals and tell herself that she wouldn't rest until she had won a lot of clients. And she would see it as a competition.

But the good news is that the feminine energy must not be entirely covered to use the masculine energy. There are situations where feminine energy is needed more than masculine energy. Below are examples of those situations:

1: You need feminine energy in moments of vulnerability

Children are pretty frustrating to deal with. A two-year-old would not hesitate to turn down the house if given a chance. The masculine energy in this situation would go straight to punishment, authoritative words, and warning. In contrast, the feminine energy would try to show the child the right way to do things. Not because the feminine power doesn't allow us to speak gently but because women see beauty in almost everything they see.

In this case, they would take the child's imperfection as an excuse for their behavior.

But what if some children already feel small and scared? It would be hard on them if masculine energy is used in this case. Still, we need masculine energy to deal with more stubborn children. The point is that feminine energy should be used when there is no threat from a child's personality.

2: You need feminine energy when there is a need to speak

Speaking up when you are expected to be silent is seen by society as a sign of masculine energy. Still, the truth is, without us women, life may be too risky. As women, we must speak because our words heal, save lives, encourage, empower and strengthen the weak. A woman with solid masculine energy knows the right words to make a vulnerable person more confident because she knows what it means to be vulnerable.

3: You need the feminine energy to prompt you in to receiving

Our masculine energy is protective of our ego, while our feminine energy seeks opportunities for more comfort. Suppose I need a specific amount of money to purchase a machine to help me work. In that case, my masculine energy tells me to go out there, work for it and not ask anyone for help. But my feminine energy tells me to receive support if someone is willing to help me. At the same time, my feminine energy would intuitively choose whom to receive help from. That's just super. This would allow me to channel my energy into other pressing issues.

4: You need the feminine energy to help spark your creativity

In the previous chapter, I talked about the nurturing aspect of the woman. And I specifically talked about how women beautifully nurture plants, especially flowers or a garden. This has been used today to show love to the opposite sex. The same woman needs to experience her feminine energy.

Creativity is also seen in the musical voices of women, the beautiful paintings, and the mouth-watering pots of food that women make. These are natural gifts that the feminine energy, and when used properly, they always yield results.

It's a beautiful thing that society now appreciates women's writing and painting skills. A few years ago, painting and writing were considered taboo for women. So women had to go under the umbrella of their husbands to get published or remain anonymous.

In the recent series 'Bridgerton,' lady Whistledown is an anonymous name for young Penelope Featherington, the most popular newspaper writer. She knew that if she revealed herself, her career would end.

Thankfully, today's women are seen as an embodiment of talent and skill. I heard a rumor that women write better stories, and I do not know how true it is, but I've read beautiful stories from women. The feminine energy is, indeed, powerful.

5: It would help if you had the feminine energy to support other women like you.

One of the beautiful things about the famous cartoon network animation, 'Power puff girls,' is how much the three girls supported each other. It's a cartoon for kids, but it holds a special meaning. That is what feminine energy should do. The ability of women to support each other in the world can be overwhelming.

I want to think that a woman as powerful as Mary Slessor used a large chunk of her feminine energy to stop the killing of twins. And I can't help but think that she was supported by many women who felt as passionate about it as she did. When women gather, reasoning, compassion, empathy, gratitude, and everything that comes with the feminine energy sparks the need for these women to create solutions when it seems there aren't. They create paths on blocked roads. Women understand the power of femininity and easily connect with themselves and other women. This becomes a safe place for women to share their pains, worries, and victories.

THE NEGATIVE EFFECT OF THE FEMININE ENERGY

1. A Lack of Active Participation

Women with intense feminine energy would rather see work as a contribution. She would see her little effort as an enormous contribution to the company because she probably thinks her boss would appreciate her. When she tries to convince people to be her clients, and they disagree, she smiles and moves on, telling herself that she will get better clients somewhere else. This is because the feminine part of women lets us listen more than we speak.

The difference between feminine and masculine energy in this situation is that feminine energy persuades and uses copywriting techniques to win customers. In contrast, feminine energy appreciates the customers' will. The feminine energy says, "I understand it is a choice." In contrast, the masculine energy says, " I will create the feeling of not wanting to miss out in the mind of this person." While being a good listener and an accommodative person is good, it could be a red flag for a person who needs active participation at work.

2. The Dependence Effect

Because feminine energy is inclined toward receiving, it could be a big challenge if a woman decides to lean overly on that energy. We all need to be independent, whether male or female. This is because as much as people would love to help us, they need to be given the space to support themselves and their families.

It's easier for a woman to begin to lean too much on her energy than for a man to. That is why masculine energy is there to balance things. Let me emphasize this more clearly; every human has masculine and feminine energies, but we all need to know when to use them.

3. The Abuse Effect

Have you ever wondered why some women keep returning to an abusive person? We get beaten, talked down on, and ignored, but we still find ourselves in the company of whoever does that to us. This is because some women have leaned too much on feminine energy. The feminine energy gives off a woman's receiving, compassionate, understanding, and loving part. This makes her overlook these parts to the point she gets so used to them that they become the routine in her life.

When humans get used to anything that affects their emotions or brain, a coping mechanism is developed to the disadvantage of anyone involved.

The worst thing about this is that it's harder for women because of our natural soft nature.

4. The Sacrifice Effect

One of the most substantial parts of feminine power is the ability of a woman to put other people before herself. This is good quality, but it cannot be good when it's time to put herself first. Sarah was one of the best staff in the company where she worked, and Maya was seen as her competition, but she never had a problem with it. As usual, she always told everyone that working in a top-rated company was a privilege.

But she knew deep within her that she needed to work harder because the time when some employees would be laid off was coming.

She needed this promotion to save enough money to further her education and provide for her younger siblings, who depended on her. But she couldn't help but pity Maya, the first of five children. She found Maya seated on the toilet in the ladies restroom with tears on her face. After much persuasion, Maya told her she didn't want to lose the opportunity.

Sarah felt great compassion for Maya and gave her business plan to Maya to present to their boss. At the same time, she lied that she had mistakenly dropped hers at the bus station. She knew their boss couldn't afford to lose her, so she was confident about it.

He was furious, but he had no choice but to promote Maya, who became Sarah's senior colleague. Maya became rude after some days and even went ahead to put Sarah in big trouble, which forced her boss to send her away.

It is not wrong to make sacrifices for people, but it is better to ask ourselves what we would lose for the gift. Feminine energy is good energy, but it costs Sarah her job in this case.

SIGNS OF HIGH FEMININE ENERGY

1. You are appreciated.

The deepest desire of every human being is to feel loved and valued. If given to a person, this feeling makes them enter into their office to give to or acknowledge a person. I have been told several times that I'm a good listener and adviser. This is because I am built to feel what others feel, especially in bad situations. This energy alone endears any person to a woman. People suddenly begin to gear towards us; they open up and find solace in being vulnerable.

Anyone who opens up to a person has indirectly sent a message that says; I have noticed your feminine energy, and it makes me feel safe enough to be open with you.

2. Give yourself lovely treats.

A woman will always seek ways to take care of her body and develop herself beautifully, provided she has solid feminine energy. I have found myself looking up lovely dress styles, hairstyles, body creams, prices of vacation trips, and so on. It feels fun, and it is fun. So I put on my feminine energy and bounce off to get self-love injections. Do it, woman. You have energy!

3. You love deeply

A woman deeply in love with her child, job, or husband has no business thinking about negativity because feminine energy gives her the positive strength she needs to go on. As a woman who does not find love hard, I appreciate life from my standpoint.

That is what feminine energy can do to us women. When we love ourselves, we would love anyone else.

4. People call you "mother".

I have had to stop adults like me from calling me a mother, and I often wonder why anyone would think I am already a mom. Still, after learning about feminine energy, I started to reply to them with, 'child!.'

There's a kind of connection between the people around me and me. A motherly and deep soul connection that makes them trust me.

CHAPTER THREE

THINGS THAT DRAIN YOUR FEMININE ENERGY

Claiming your feminine energy is the heart of your happiness and everything that concerns you. Many things can drain your feminine power and rid you of the joy of embracing your feminine side. Identifying and letting go of these things is crucial in this journey.
Before I go on, let me quickly reiterate that human beings have both feminine and masculine energies.

The word feminine means female, and the word masculine means male. But feminine and masculine energies do not mean female and male energy.
Unlike what we know, masculine energy is strict, logical, direct, and structured. It is the energy we put in motion whenever we want to carry out tasks and do our jobs effectively.

While feminine energy is the soft, fluid, sweet energy, it is the energy we put in motion to feel and explore our sides more.

As a result of conditioning, society has had a way of attributing masculine energy to men and feminine energy to females. But this doesn't seem right. We all need these energies to navigate through life's course effectively.

The weeks after I ditched the excellent old masculine energy I had carried with me all my life were some of the darkest weeks in my life. I constantly doubted myself and my decision to let my feminine nature be at the forefront of my life.

I learned this just as I stepped into the light of my feminine journey. In the race to tap into your full potential as a beautiful, bold, and strong woman, some things will weigh you down, and here's a list of them and how to overcome them.

Restricting Yourself From Experiencing.

A way to drain yourself of your feminine energy is to restrict yourself, intentionally or not, from experiencing it. Many of us do this either because we feel that being in our masculine essence makes us feel more assertive, and we exude more power. Other women do it unconsciously. If you fall into this category, it is okay.

You need to understand that stepping into your feminine energy does not mean throwing your masculine energy out of your life. It only means allowing yourself to be more intuitive, soft, and fluid.

You should be more in touch with your emotional, physical, social, and mental sides, exploring each like the wind does to the petals of a flower. So, even on one tough side, you are gentle on the other. Embracing your feminine energy does not mean you are weak. We are only trying to create a balance. A necessary balance.

Staying in Environments That Value Masculine Traits Than Feminine Ones.

Staying in environments that reward masculinity has been more harmful than helpful. This only makes women disconnect from their feminine sides and embrace acting, talking, and behaving like men to thrive in society. Talks upon talks have been on for years about feminism and how women should be equal to men. Over time, the conversation moved from "Women should be equal to men" to "women should try to be like men." But this is not what we want. We do not want to behave like men.

The false mentality that being masculine makes women stronger pulls the feminine energies of women further into oblivion. Due to this, many women still find it hard to strike a balance. Most of them have followed in the footsteps of men to prove to society that what a man can do, a woman can do better.

And in the end, they feel hardened, uptight, and rough. If this is you, it's alright. You can make amends. The first step you need to take is to understand that a human has both energies. It is essential to be in touch with both to avoid consequences that result from the negligence of the other. Do not allow your environment to influence you into thinking that behaving like a man is strength. It is killing your feminine energy with your permission.

Seeing Your Feminine Parts as Weak:

Most of us have had misconceptions about how behaving like a lady makes you weak and behaving like a man makes you strong. This has caused many women to hide their feminine energies and act like men–take up masculine roles and be more around men to feel as powerful as they seem. This causes our masculine energy to be more active than the feminine, which is unhealthy, as you should know. But it requires the willingness to drop those shackles and be truly free. Your masculine energy serves as a container for your feminine energy. It is hollow and craves a certain amount of feminine power for the balance to be felt.

It's the same with feminine energy. You cannot fully operate with just your feminine energy. It needs a balance, or it may risk being abused and trampled upon by society.

Both have to be kept in balance to ensure effective and healthy living as a woman; to know this is to know peace.

Holding Onto Memories from Traumatic and Abusive Experiences in the Past.

Ugly memories from the past, which can include emotional, physical, or sexual abuse, can cause your feminine energy level to decrease by a significant percentage. This could be due to the nature of the abuse, which made you feel like it happened because you are a woman–"if I were a man, maybe, just maybe, I wouldn't have gone through that." And so, you unconsciously embrace your masculine energy more because you feel safer and more in control there. I understand perfectly, and I relate. But remember, as a woman, being in your masculine energy always leaves you wanting more. It almost feels like something is missing, but you don't know what it is. It's your feminine energy! I mean, behaving like a "man" sure feels great until you are in a gathering of women that makes you feel out of place. It's like a void you know you have to fill. If this is your case, I understand.

You can still step right into your feminine energy. The process may be challenging, but really, what is accessible? Winks! You will have to revisit your past and find and heal old wounds. Think of it this way; these experiences are like thrusts that have deeply penetrated the core of your feminine energy. They have created holes that need to be filled. After the filling comes recovery and healing.

So, filling to recovery to healing.

It's a cycle that must be completed to step back into your feminine energy once more.

Low Feminine Energy During Childhood.

Let me tell you a quick story. I am the firstborn of my family. Before birth, my parents bought me a truckload of male clothes and accessories. They were so sure that I was going to turn out as a boy. This certainty was so much that everyone in the family, both nuclear and extended, waited with excited hearts for my arrival. My mother refused to go for a scan to check the gender of the baby she was carrying. She wanted a pleasant surprise!

When I eventually came as a girl, they always projected masculine energy toward me. I grew in the heat of this energy, and slowly, I began to embrace manliness unconsciously, and I was drawn to things that the male gender would.

These experiences drained my feminine energy even before I realized it was there! If this is also your case, I need you to know that you are not alone. If I could step out of it and come to the knowledge of my feminine energy, so can you. It is never too late to discover your feminine energy because when we eventually do, we begin to see significant changes in how we live our lives and relate to others. We become more emotional, empathic, affectionate, and warm.

And these changes would reflect in every aspect of our lives–socially, physically, mentally, and emotionally.

Never Asking for Help.

This is another strong force that drains feminine energy.

The first thing I want you to understand here is that there is nothing wrong with asking for help. The masculine energy loves to accomplish tasks and get things done, which is why it is the doing energy.

Not asking for help means you have just your masculine energy active and must drop into your feminine as soon as possible. This takes me down memory lane. Long before I discovered my feminine energy. I went for a mountain climbing exercise with some of my friends. On our way, something pricked the dorsal part of my feet, but I tried my best not to shout. As we got closer and closer to the mountain, I discovered I was bleeding. Nobody noticed. I didn't call out for help until someone saw me and offered to help nurse the wound fast so we could catch up with the others. I vehemently refused and kept telling him I was fine and it was a minor injury. But he eventually persuaded me to rest my back against one of the rocks while he looked at the wound. The truth is, it was profound, and I needed immediate medical help. He had to call the others, and together, they carried me back to where the car was and rushed me to a nearby clinic.

Now, imagine for a second that nobody had noticed me. I wouldn't have asked for help, and the case might have been more severe than it was. I didn't ask for help because I thought it would make me weak and dependent. I wouldn't say I liked depending on anybody, but in the true sense, I was getting weaker and weaker by not asking for help. Do you see the drill? There are times when you actually cannot do it alone, like that incident! We all need people in one way or the other to help us achieve one thing or another. Understanding this is the first step when dropping into your feminine energy. So, as women, let us normalize asking for help when needed.

It doesn't make us less human. It acknowledges that we're stuck, but we appreciate resources that would assist us in getting out.

Comparing Yourself to Men.

There is nothing positive about the comparison, and it only makes us feel not up to the task. Sometimes, we might beat ourselves up just because we have not attained the height that our male counterparts have.

Then we begin to create silly assertions, like "if I was a man, I would have done this or gotten this, or had this." In my case, I compared myself to my colleagues at work, fellow singers in the choir, and prosaists in the writing field. Comparing yourself with just any gender screams insecurity, but comparing yourself with the male gender indicates explicitly that your feminine energy is being drained.

We must first understand that comparison has never made anyone better at solving this. It only creates hate and jealousy, which goes against what we represent as women with thriving feminine energies.

The second way is by tapping into our power. As Black women, we have a scarily generous amount of energy embedded in us, but most of us do not know this. And as a result, we do not tap into it. When we tap into our power, it prevents us from wallowing in self-doubt and self-pity. We realize that everyone has a different pace and destination from the next person's, and we go on with our journey peacefully with this knowledge.

Neglecting Your Body Signals.

As women, our bodies are naturally created to be soft and crave warmth and care. Sometimes, when we over-work ourselves or when our bodies have reached their working limits, they send signals that notify us of stress, tiredness, or hunger. Usually, we should give our bodies what they want at this point. But some of us decide to turn deaf ears to those signals, suppress them and forge ahead. This is a factor that drains your feminine energy. Not listening to your body signifies that your feminine energy is being drained and in need of refilling. The feminine energy makes us pay attention to our feelings and thoughts and needs to attend to them as fast as we can. When we do all these, we find that we are more productive and still in touch with ourselves. This is the balance that we preach!

Neglecting Self-care:

Self-care is the process that involves looking after your mind, body, and spirit. It fills your mind with information that empowers your inner and outer self and opens you up to growth. As women, self-care should be our priority, and we should pay attention to how we look, sound, behave and act. When we realize we don't care about how our hair looks or smells, we do not care about significant changes in or on our bodies; we do not care about the kind of clothes we wear, then that is a cue that tells us that there is a drop in the level of our feminine energy and that we need to recharge our batteries and start paying attention to ourselves more.

Not Accepting Yourself.

Women have been taught to conform to societal beliefs plastered on us like tags. Over the years, these tags have become too heavy for us to carry, and the weight causes our authentic selves to drown and then disappear. Then, we take on attributes that are not ours to own, making us forget who we are.

Society wants the average woman to be a certain way, but all women cannot be the same. We cannot all have flat tummies, pointed noses, straight legs, and round hips. We are all differently beautiful, and the moment you allow these projections to get to you, your feminine energy depreciates. You no longer feel comfortable in your skin, you no longer feel beautiful in cornrows, and you don't want to see your reflection in the mirror anymore because you think there is a particular way you should be.

All these things would make you criticize yourself every time, and your mental energy begins to rise against your feminine self.

What to do to rise above these things?

Girl, love yourself. You have to love yourself first before expecting love from anybody. Own your body, love it, cherish it, and care for it. We look the way we look because that was exactly how we were created to look. We should understand that we are unique creations and don't have to look like anybody to prove that we're worth all the love, care, and attention we deserve. We don't have to look a particular way to smash goals and look after ourselves. It's all in us!

Lack of Women Around You.

As humans, we are naturally attracted to both men and women, as the case may be, depending on the ways they connect or resonate with us. But, as a woman, if the only females in your life are your mother and your sister, you are right on your way to draining your feminine energy. Why? Because masculine energy has been presented as stereotypically masculine, and men embody this energy. Surrounding yourself with men only spikes your male power and leaves your feminine energy dormant. Consequently, you will even start to behave like them, model their characteristics and–pay attention to this last point!– start saying what they want to hear. Yes. Women are built to be soft, and masculine energy is penetrative.

When it takes its toll on you, you begin to talk in the way these men want you to, leaving no chance to say what you want.

It would help if you learned how to surround yourself with women to create a balance. Visit women empowering programs, go to women-themed picnics, and join a women's community. You will realize that when you do all these, you will start to feel more because you are surrounded by like-minded beings. Your sweet, sensitive and tender parts will find the light once more.

WAYS TO REFILL YOUR FEMININE ENERGY

- **Find out what drained the energy in the first place.**

There are many reasons women experience a drop in their feminine energy level. For it to be refilled, we must understand why it got reduced.

Is it a result of physical or emotional assault? Were you raped as a child? Were you exposed to too much masculine energy growing up as a child? Did you grow up in a male-dominated family? Were you constantly shamed for being a woman?

If you fall into this category, then there is one thing I want you to know. These experiences that you have are projections from other people. They do not define you! I know it can be hard to swallow, but if you want to take back your feminine energy, you have to let go of what drained it! You have to understand that those who made you feel like you have to be like a man to succeed only made statements that they thought were right. But you can choose what is right and what is not. Their thoughts shouldn't mean anything to you. You should not be carrying a load that's not yours all your life because someone said you should. Drop it! I know you feel the hurt, and the pain still seems fresh, but there is a way you can heal, and the first step is putting all of these experiences behind you and allowing yourself to open up.

This way, your feminine energy can seep through you once again. It is a slow but sure way.

- **Be more conscious of yourself.**

You can be more conscious by paying attention to the little things. What do you like doing? What do you want to eat? How you love to prepare your meals.

Where you like to go? What do you enjoy doing most? How you laugh when you read your favorite book? What makes you smile? What lights up your soul? Which songs do you like listening to? What you are most comfortable in. Knowing and keeping track of these things is a sure way to refill your feminine energy. It ushers you into a state of confidence, knowing yourself from the inside out. This way, you're able to express yourself more.

- **Take care of yourself.**

This goes on to say, love yourself. Let your love for yourself be reflected in how you do things. How you eat. The way you talk. The way you act. Let it remember in your conversations with yourself and with other people. If you are a woman that loves to feel her naturalness, take care of your skin; use products that align with your skin type. Wear your hair with pride and show yourself off with enthusiasm. Wear clothes that you are most comfortable in. Walk with unarguable confidence and an energetic gait. Take yourself out on love dates, buy gifts, wear lipstick, embrace receiving, go for spa treatments, and go on tours. These sweet little "nothings" go a long way to recharging your feminine battery and setting you up for endless positivity.

- **Surround yourself with powerful women.**

As women, we like to see ourselves together in oneness because we exude this feeling of power. There is also the freedom to feel vulnerable, and we can share our encounters, feelings, and needs without feeling out of place. Start surrounding yourself with high-spirited women. Women who are always lit and would not hesitate to share some light with you when yours goes out, women who are empowering in every area of life. You can have them as mentors, friends, acquaintances, and colleagues. The sure thing is that having them around you opens you up to as much feminine energy as you need to steer through life and win in all aspects.

CHAPTER FOUR

THE WOMAN WHO LOVES HERSELF WHOLLY

"Love yourself first, and everything else falls into line. You really have to love yourself to get anything done in this world." —Lucille Ball.

One sure recipe to truly dive into your feminine energy and embrace it is to love yourself wholly. A woman who loves herself completely will blossom and flourish in her feminine energy.

Low self-esteem, insecurities, and self-hate will stop at nothing to keep a woman from reaching her true potential. I am a living example of this. There used to be a time when I was my enemy, and I looked around me and wondered how the other women lived beautiful and successful lives. Now, I don't even mean women I saw on TV and the internet. I mean women from my hood. I wanted to know how they could get out of their head for a start and how they began flourishing and wearing their feminine energy like a sweet perfume. I wanted that more than anything. I want to put it out there that you will never be able to achieve anything unless you desire it hard enough.

What held me down wasn't the masculine energy I adopted growing up. Of course, it was part of the problem, but it wasn't the whole deal. A massive chunk of my stagnancy came from the inside, and it came from the fact that I didn't love myself wholly. Getting out of that wretched frame of mind was crucial to my growth as a successful woman who felt good about herself.

I will share some practical tips that helped me transform from a woman with low self-esteem to a woman very much in love with all parts of herself.

Trust Yourself To Make Good Decisions.

As a woman who is out to take charge of her life, you have to trust yourself to make decisions that will lead you to your desired destination in life. If you are in constant doubt about your decision-making skills, you will never fully make any progress. You have to believe in yourself and that you can reshape your life.

No one knows you more than you know yourself. You should know what is best for you and be responsible for every decision. It is one thing to make decisions for yourself, while it is another to take responsibility for those decisions.

Also, starting your day with affirmations can strengthen your self-worth and self-love, and they fill you with positive energy and transform your pessimistic thinking patterns into optimistic ones.

One of the daily affirmations I used to chant is, *"I Make Good Decisions."*

I like this one because it is short, simple, direct, and compelling. It did wonders for me, and I'm sure it will also work for you.

If you doubt your decision-making, you should try out this affirmation or curate one yourself. Write down what you want to be plastered across your heart. When you are finished, pick it up every morning when you wake up and read it out to yourself.

Your Worth is not Measured by How Your Body Looks.

This is a critical point to note. Your body outlook is not directly proportional to your worth and relevance as a woman trying to embrace her feminine energy. Sis, know this and know peace. No matter what you look like, be it a size 0 or 100, it has nothing to do with your value.

Your self-worth and self-love start with the mind, which cannot be measured by the size of your breast or your ass. It has to be cultivated inside of you, and then slowly but surely, it would reflect on the outside for people to see.

If you have been measuring your importance in this world by how you look in front of the mirror, then you are doing a vile, terrible thing. You have to come off it! Come off the self-pity and degenerating self-image you have in your head. It's time for you to begin loving yourself unconditionally.

Putting Yourself First.

There's only one position for you to be in your life, and that is the first. You have no business with being second or third. So long as it's your life, you have every right to take the front seat.

Stop putting others before yourself when it's going to be detrimental to you, especially when the person isn't worth it. Since we are women, society has brainwashed us into thinking that we must always put others before ourselves, for example, our children, which is not a bad idea. I trust you not to take this out of context. We have grown so accustomed to putting others before ourselves that we are blind in deciphering those who are worthy of it and those who are not. Most people are going to take advantage of us without batting an eye. So to prevent it, we have to put ourselves first.

Don't feel bad about doing this. Eventually, it's going to be worth it. A woman who wants to step into her feminine energy always has to put herself at the forefront of her physical, mental, and emotional well-being.

When I began doing those mentioned above, I recorded a tremendous upgrade in my life. I was more in love with myself, and I was flourishing mentally.

All you have to do is desire it hard enough. Do you want to change? Get up and make the change happen.

HOW WOMEN WHO LOVE THEMSELVES UNDERSTAND THEIR FEMININE ENERGY

Now that I have gotten the "self-love" aspect, I will talk about how loving ourselves as women can help us better understand our feminine energy.

Loving yourself gives you an edge over the next woman trying to understand and embrace her feminine energy without attempting to cultivate self-love. Now, I do not mean that there is a competition on who can love herself better. When you love yourself, understanding your feminine energy becomes a piece of cake.

Claiming your feminine energy is simply riding with the tranquil flow of your life and accepting your divine soothing power. It may sound spiritual to you, just like it first did to me. You cannot hop on this bus if you don't love yourself.

Here are some reasons why loving yourself helps you understand your feminine energy.

You Cannot Give What You Don't Have.

If you do not have a love for yourself, it will be nearly impossible to love your feminine energy, and when you do not love your feminine energy, you will be unable to manifest it. Remember that your feminine energy is riding or going with the tranquil flow of your life, embracing your inner peace. You cannot find that peace or tranquility if you possess no love. It's that simple.

During my formative years of embracing my feminine energy, I almost made the mistake of diving into the energy without first taking the time to develop a fondness for myself. I wanted to run before I could crawl, which is frankly not right.

Feminine energy is kind, empathetic, emotional, patient, and genuine. It isn't selfish, and it is far from that. Refusing to love yourself is more than being selfish. When you're selfish, you cannot be anything feminine energy stands for and can certainly never understand how it works.

Feminine Energy Influences Your Attitude.

The attitude of a woman who doesn't love herself is pretty glaring. You will see that she doesn't prioritize her own needs, pays little to no attention to her appearance, and doesn't eat right. She settles for the barest minimum in whatever relationship she finds herself in. Now, these are not all of it. There are dozens of more attitudes, but I won't mention all.

When a woman tries to step into her feminine energy without tackling these issues, she will be left stuck because feminine emery influences your attitude. No progress will be made if you've got a bad mood. The feminine energy does not promote a lousy attitude. It needs a sane, clear mind to function correctly. Loving yourself is the first step to achieving this.

You Exude Your Feminine Energy by Loving Yourself.

When you love yourself, you are more likely to exude the right vibes and all the benefits of embracing your feminine energy. It is just not enough to read a few articles online and decide that you want to be more connected to your feminine energy. It would help if you also did the basics, like leaving behind self-hate, depression, and low self-esteem. You cannot fully step into your power if you've got such baggage. You can never fully exude your feminine energy when you don't love yourself. One of the things that feminine energy lets us do is pamper ourselves. I read an article once that had a long list of self-care routines that we, as women, should do if we want to increase our feminine energy.

The list contained things like; drinking herbal tea, going to the salon, getting professional pedicures and manicures, having a warm bath, keeping a journal, e.t.c. Frankly, this looks like a bunch of things some women who are in love with themselves would do, not those who aren't.

HOW SELF-LOVE INFLUENCES THE ENERGY

Self-love is essential and is the most crucial foundation of any relationship. Self-love means having respect and esteem for your happiness. Self-love influences how you handle your life daily. It includes how you interact with people, how you handle the different obstacles you face, and your physical and mental health, basically how well you take care of yourself.

In college, I had a boyfriend I loved very much. At that time, he was the center of my world. We have been dating for at least six months. All my friends knew him, but I met very few of his friends.

We were from the same little town and lived there with our families. I was low-key fantasizing about the two of us getting married after we got out of college. Everything at that time seemed perfect, but as life would have it, things were bound to go wrong no matter how right we wanted.

He was cheating on me with a girl from his class. She wasn't just a girl from his town, she lived in his neighborhood back home, and they had been dating since high school. I had never felt a pain in my chest so intense before. I had built my present around him and was slowly making my future around him.

I had little to no self-love or self-care going on at that time. Because I was so engrossed in everything that pertained to the boyfriend. The breakup made me suffer a lot.

Then, a friend gave me a much-needed lecture on self-love and how I was supposed to cultivate it. I was too distraught to care about anything other than my broken heart, but I listened to her anyway.

I started taking good care of myself physically, emotionally, and mentally. That way, moving on from the breakup became easier.

Self-love made me realize that it was his loss, not mine, and it opened my eyes to the fact that I was a fantastic person who deserved the best and not the barest minimum. I was studying and researching self-love and self-worth, constantly reminding myself that I was enough for that. Towards the end of the first month, I did not have a single iota of self-pity.

The unfortunate man returned begging, talking about how he had realized that it was me that he truly loved. The audacity for me sometimes!

It wasn't until many years later, when I suffered yet another heartbreak, that I discovered the concept of feminine energy. I was at a low point in my life; all the acts of self-love that I had cultivated over the years were slowly washing down the drain. I had just had a bad breakup with someone I was practically going to get married to. No amount of self-care routine could get me past that one. And so, I began embracing my feminine energy and made the mistake of living out self-love, and boy, was that a grave mistake!

How to Love Yourself and Influence Your Feminine Energy.

Start a Self-love Journal.

A self-love journal is done to discover more about yourself and to reflect on your thoughts and actions. It is different from the other kinds of journaling.
Starting a self-love journal is a guaranteed way to help you love yourself because you can discover things about yourself that you didn't even know were there.

Try meditating.

Practicing meditation as a form of self-love helps you to get rid of negative energies around you and allows you to be honest and vulnerable with yourself. It also gives you a chance to focus on having internal ease. Having inner peace will bring clarity, and you will accept yourself for who you are; thereby allowing you to be able to step into your feminine energy.

Try Yoga.

Yoga is one of the best methods of self-love. The benefits of yoga can be both mental and physical. You can focus your senses on deep internal healing when you practice yoga. It is excellent when you have a lot of negative thoughts that are constantly weighing you down. Yoga has been proven effective for people dealing with depression, anxiety, etc. Yoga also benefits you physically because it can help you keep fit and improve your strength and flexibility.

Use all your senses.

Using all your senses when practicing self-care can be pretty beneficial. As we all know, our senses consist of our eyes, ears, nose, mouth, and skin. A completely different self-care routine can be drafted for each of the reasons or coupled with other sensory activities.

Eyes (Seeing)

Basically, for the eyes, the trick is to indulge yourself in activities that include using your visuals. For example, drawing, seeing a movie, reading a book, e.t.c.

Ears (Hearing)

This has to do with sound, so listening to great music, meditative sounds or even a motivational podcast can help.

Nose (Smelling)

Aromatherapy has been proven to be an excellent combat fighter for stress relief. It triggers the relaxation response that is needed for self-care. It is a complete healing treatment that uses natural plant extracts to promote wellness and good health. Some unique scents for stress relief, such as lavender, Jasmine, sandalwood, rose, bergamot e.t.c are known to promote relaxation and increase focus and feelings of peace.

Mouth (Tasting)

The mouth is primarily associated with communication and eating, and of course, kissing.

Practice Mindful Communication.

This is filtering your language and cutting down on swear words because they do nothing but pollute your soul. You have to focus more on using your speech to say meaningful things. Use it to affirm greatness in your life and not talk down on yourself. When you communicate with others, be careful about what you say and who you tell them to. Evil communication corrupts good manners, they say. Speak no evil, my friend.

Practice Mindful Eating.

When was the last time you savored your meal? When was the last time you ate as you tried to taste the flavor and texture in every bite? We live in a fast-paced world, and thus we have been conditioned to eat just as fast as the earth spins, but you can learn to be mindful of your meals.

Eat slowly and thoroughly and avoid all forms of distractions. Be invested in the meal in front of you. Put down that phone and focus on what's on your plate. Not only does mindful eating help you pay more attention to the meal you have in front of you, but it also helps you to stop unnecessary meals. When you are mindful of what you take into your body, you will consciously watch out for being overfed and practically cut off all forms of binge eating.

(iii) **Only Kiss The Right People:** This may sound silly, but it needs to be spoken about. How do you know a person is right? Time. Time will tell. Until then, keep your lips sealed. It is wrong to let everyone who comes your way have their way with you. Waiting for the right time to get involved with the right person is a form of self-care. Let people deserve it. Let them earn that kiss!

Skin (Feeling): The skin is versatile, and many activities can be done as self-care—for example, a skincare routine or physical touch for massage therapy.

(i) What better way to express self-love than to take complete care of your skin and do all the right things to keep it glowing? What could be better than having clear skin? Look for a good skincare routine and stick to it. Taking care of your skin is one of the most fantastic forms of self-love and one you will always thank yourself for doing.

(ii) Going to a massage parlor for a massage, as they say, is one of the traditional forms of self-care and one of the oldest. Studies have shown that a massage can reduce cortisol, a significant stress hormone, by a whopping 31%! A good massage will reduce stress levels and leave you cheerful and delighted.

Ultimately, it is worth noting that all the self-care activities mentioned above will only promote your feminine energy if you consciously decide to let it do so. Many women have found the tranquility of life they so much desire by adhering to these rules. If they can do it, I'm sure you can too.

CHAPTER FIVE

FEAR AS AN HINDRANCE TO FEMININE ENERGY

"Do the thing you fear, and the death of fear is certain."'
— *Ralph Waldo Emerson*

Fear is a barrier that keeps women away from loving themselves. Our femininity is a vast ocean of power that we can utilize, but with fear standing as a hindrance between us and embracing our feminine energy, there is only so much that we can do to be the woman we want to be.

Fear being a hindrance to our feminine energy is not emphasized enough. There are several reasons why this is even a thing, ranging from the fear of what others would think, overdoing it (over embracing our feminine essence), fear of failing, e.t.c. I once had a client who was scared of embracing her feminine energy. She worked at a corporate company and had a burning desire to become the head of the HR department. She thought embracing her feminine energy would make her lose her chance of getting the position, but after counseling her, I could penetrate her mind to see the bigger picture. I made her understand that embracing her feminine energy did not mean completely getting rid of her masculine energy but allowing the two points to operate hand in hand. In no time, she got the promotion she wanted. Now, I'm not saying that embracing your feminine energy without fear as a hindrance would automatically get you in whatever position you desire. It doesn't work that way. But stepping into your power is a sure catalyst for greatness.

SURROUND YOURSELF WITH PEOPLE THAT REFLECT WHO YOU WANT TO BE

To reach your peak, step into your energy and put asunder everything that causes you to be afraid. You have to surround yourself with people that reflect who you want to be.

You have to be friends who share the same train of thoughts with you. Of course, they may have their view of life, which may be different from yours, but it is advisable to surround yourself with people who are taking the same path in life as you. This is just the first step, and there are several of them.

Surrounding yourself with like-minded individuals
Surrounding yourself with people that reflect who you want to be
Surrounding yourself with successful people

If, for example, you have picked out Mitchell Obama as the woman you want to emulate, you will have to feed frequently on whatever information you find about her.

Spending time reading everything that has either been written or inspired by her and listening to her speak. You do not want to do too much, so you don't appear creepy.

You have to make them role models. Remember that energies are contagious.

"But what if they are famous people thousands of miles away from me?"

Sitting next to a person is not the only way to surround yourself with them. That's why every day, I am grateful for the gift of technology. In our modern world, it has become easy to stay connected to people far away from you and those you do not have access to. It would help if you utilized every means to keep related to your role models and high-value friends (I don't say money but in goals, aspirations, and the go-getter mindset!)

Doing this can eliminate all forms of fear, and it no longer becomes a hindrance. It is just like a child who was once scared of petting a dog but suddenly became courageous after seeing someone else do it.

THE WORLD IS YOURS FOR YOUR TAKING

Sometimes, I make myself sad by thinking about women in marginalized countries who may never have the chance to discover their feminine energy, much less embrace it. It is truly saddening, and that is why I get angry when I see women privileged to gain this knowledge but so choked up in their comfort zone that they do not bother to want more out of life. Such women are their problems, like a faulty car that must be pushed before it starts.

These women do not understand that the world is for their taking.

I once had a married woman come to me for counseling. She had been married for fifteen years and was a stay-at-home morning who never had a job and depended on her husband for everything. Fair enough, the husband raked in hundreds of dollars every year, catering to her needs.

Regardless, this woman had a need tugging in her chest, and that was to be something more. To be a woman who had a life outside of her marriage, outside of her children.

Of course, she loved her children but also wanted to love something else. She tried to love herself. I paid keen attention to her story as she relayed it to me. I could tell that she had been thinking about this for years and that the only thing that had hindered her from taking that first step was none other than fear.

She feared being so engrossed in herself that she forgot about her family, which was absurd to be before. In reality, embracing your feminine energy makes you excel better in all forms of relationships that you have going on for you. What's better is that it makes other people draw closer to you. Embracing your feminine energy will not chase people away from you. I walked this woman through the journey of being a high-valued female, and now, she thanks me every other day for taking her up.

Girls, the world is yours to take. According to Beyonce, who runs the world? I'm sure you got the answer.

BE PREPARED TO FAIL.

Nothing is certain in life. There are always two endpoints to whatever project you embark on in life:

It fails
It succeeds

There is no in-between, so you have to be prepared to get frustrated, lose your mind, get angry, and want to give in, but you must overcome those urges because it is all part of the process. Nothing good comes easy, they say. You will have pitfalls, but remaining consistent and rising above every challenge each time they come your way will make you better than the next woman who gives up after one attempt.

BE PREPARED TO SUCCEED

Success will not fall into your laps; in that case, you will not be able to fully embrace your feminine energy if you are not putting in the effort to succeed on this journey. The greater your preparation, the more confident and less afraid you will feel.

One time in college, I was going through some family issues that made me slack in my academic life. It was so bad that I could not study for a particular course ahead of an examination. I remember getting ready for school that day and knowing fully well that I would fail because I had put in no effort to study for the test. When the results came out, I had a D. I was pretty shaken because I had expected an F all along. You may not be so lucky to get a D out of life if you do not prepare properly for the challenges you will face. A good result will not magically manifest if you do not plan to make it happen. Be prepared for success.

EVERYTHING YOU WANT IS ON THE OTHER SIDE OF FEAR

Cliche much? But it's the truth. Do you want to embrace your feminine energy? Cross the fence, then. Climb up the wall and jump over. Go to the other side. Everything you have ever wanted will be within your reach when you take the bold step to leap over the fence. To get what you want, you must overcome your fear.

Imagine what you can accomplish if you go ahead to get it. That new job, the new apartment, even the fine man that lives across your street! But you can't get these things because you are afraid of failing.

Everyone sometimes doubts, but a resilient person does not remain in their comfort zone. They will get up and do what needs to be done. Fear is a tremendous emotion; for some, it is a band-aid against the unknown. Fear keeps us from doing things that may cause us pain, harm, hurt, and whatnot, but we fail to realize that there is no pain and no gain.

Our role models went through one form of pain or the other before they won. It may not have been painful, but the good thing, everything in life is relative. They have been able to engrave their name on gold. They made sacrifices for their dreams. That should be enough inspiration for you, my friend. If they can do it, then you can too. The only thing that is holding you back is you.

Fear will limit you from attaining great heights. If you desire to make a difference, then you have to stop being afraid and start being in control of your life.

This is your sign to quit your hate job and pursue your dream. This is your sign of embracing your feminine side This is your sign to step into your energy. You can't let fear hold you back any longer. This is your sign of regaining control over your life. This is your sign! This is your sign!

CHAPTER SIX

EMPOWERING YOURSELF AND BOOSTING YOUR ENERGY, AND MORPHING INTO YOUR BEST SELF

We cannot all succeed when half of us are held back. We call upon our sisters around the world to be brave – to embrace the strength within themselves and realize their full potential.
-Malala Yousafzai

Taking a deliberate and conscious effort to take charge of your life is self-empowering.
Self-empowered people set goals for themselves, work towards those goals and eventually achieve the set goals.

There are numerous ways to empower yourself, from setting reasonable goals to being assertive. Below, I will take you on a few tips to help you understand what you must do to empower yourself regarding claiming your feminine energy.

Set a reasonable goal for yourself.

This is a vital tool to empower your mind and body. The plans you set are meant to motivate you. When you set unachievable goals, you set yourself up for failure. You cannot afford to continue living your life in a mediocre way. That is why you have to set realistic and achievable goals for yourself. Say, for example, you want to begin a journey of self-love. You have chosen to focus on your six senses– all at once as opposed to taking it one step at a time, for example, focusing on your understanding of sight for two weeks and then your nose for another two weeks until all the six senses have been exhausted.

You may fail when you choose to do the latter because you have refused to give your body, soul, and mind time to adjust to your new routine.

Practice Self-love.

Taking care of your needs and putting yourself first without sacrificing yourself to satisfy the needs of others is self-love. There are other definitions of this word, and we have discussed the concept of self-love in the previous chapters, but one thing that has to be duly noted is that self-love and self-care go hand in hand. Self-care is inevitable when one seeks a part in the journey of self-love. So, taking care of your body, soul and mind, mentally, physically, and emotionally can be self-empowering in unbelievable ways.

Develop a Positive Attitude.

While there might be an upside to being a pessimist (which includes but does not end with being prepared for bad times and avoiding risks that they deem unworthy of their sacrifice), the downside cannot be overlooked. Pessimists are people who always tend to believe that the worst will happen. They are void of hope and joy and try to dampen the spirits of optimistic people. They are not usually fun because they suck the joy out of everything they encounter. A positive attitude can help bring peace of mind and a sense of self-worth. Do not take for granted the peace that having a positive attitude can get you and the control you can have over your mental state.

Be Proactive.

Being proactive is taking responsibility for your life by being able to control the decisions that can be controlled rather than responding to them after it has happened. Bold people act in anticipation of future problems while still in the present. A basic example of being proactive is doing background research on a stranger before meeting with them in person.

Empowered people take action on situations before the situation even calls for it. They do not wait for things to go wrong before making them suitable. They will fix the first tiny cracks on the wall the moment they notice them and not wait till the building falls apart. It's what proactive people who are empowered do, and for someone who wants to step into her feminine energy, pro-activeness is one crucial ingredient that need not be missed or skipped.

Create a Self-concept About Yourself.

According to the Humanist Psychologist Carl Rogers, self-concept is a collection of beliefs about one's For, which is divided into three different parts, namely, self-image and ideal self, and self-esteem.

Self-image refers to how we see ourselves.
The ideal self is the person we want to be

Self-esteem is how much you value yourself.

Self-concept is the image we have of ourselves in our heads.

It is how we perceive our behaviors and characteristics to be. For example, I think that I am a sincere person. One that is brutally honest at that. It is my self-concept about myself, and it is what I feel about myself. Others may disagree, but it doesn't matter because this is what we believe about ourselves.

Your self-concept allows you to be aware of your strengths and weaknesses. It will enable you to take an inventory of your character, traits, values, and beliefs. It is empowering to have a concept about one's self because it lets you know yourself better, and the more you know yourself, the more you can set specific and worthwhile goals. It helps you understand your limitations, and you'll know what exactly you need.

I find it annoying when I question my clients' self-concepts, and then they give me a weary smile that screams, 'I have no idea, I'm sorry.' As a woman who wants to step into her energy, she must have formed an opinion about herself. Such as, when a person asks, 'Do you think you're an honest person?' you don't give a shy smile and tell them that you're not sure. You have to be assertive, which takes us to the final tip.

Be Assertive.

Assertiveness is the ability to confidently express and speak up for yourself respectfully without being hostile or invalidating other people's feelings. It is also the ability to stand up for yourself and speak of boldness and courage.

Assertiveness is a form of communication that can be learned. Most of us did not grow up able to look people in the eyes and express our needs and desires. Being assertive is an empowering characteristic because it allows you to communicate with people in a civilized and acceptable manner. A woman who wants to embrace her feminine energy has to be assertive.

BOOSTING YOUR ENERGY

Boosting your feminine energy means improving your feminine energy. I once had a client who only sorted for my services because she needed help raising her feminine energy. Once upon a time, she was a femininity enthusiast, but over time, she flopped in pursuing her feminine power and now needed me to put her back on track. With that said, this section is for women who are on the path to improving and increasing their energies.

This is for women who hunger for more. Here's your chance to be redeemed for a woman unsatisfied with the bare minimum.

There are some essential steps you have to take if you are looking to boost your energy. They include;

Reflect.

Reflection is a great way to begin improving your feminine energy. Reflecting is all about thinking deeply about something. It would help if you did this because chances are that you have been so busy with the worries of life that you have lost track of what's happening inside you. You can take out a few minutes every day to stop and reflect. To tune into your spirit.

Connect With Nature.

There's a reason nature is commonly referred to as female. (Mother Nature). I understand that not many people would be interested in grass, trees, lakes, and birds, but, to truly boost your energy, you have to engross yourself in the wonders of nature, the wonders of the world that you were born into. We are not separate from the earth. We are not at war with the planet. We are an integral part of the green ball we live in. Some people do not give a damn about a beautiful sunset, even though they should. Go out there, and gaze at the stars, the clouds, and the breathtaking beauty of these things. Be completely immersed in them because they are abundant with natural feminine energy. By doing this, you will see that you have created a sense of harmony and peace inside of you.

Listen to your intuition.

Although decisions based on intuition are frowned upon in our masculine society today, they shouldn't stop you from using them. You have been very intuitive from the start, but as you grew older, you were shut out by the masculine society, which made you keep your intuitiveness, and now, you're 30 and can't seem to find the voice of intuition anymore.

Sometimes, ask yourself when was the last time you listened to your gut feeling. Mind you, the voice of intuition can never entirely go away. It is still in you, just that it is much quieter now. Your job now is to listen carefully to it. Pay keen attention so you don't miss it. As a woman embracing her feminine energy, having her intuition intact is a plus because she can make better decisions and lead a more controlled, organized life. Your intuition could come in the form of a voice or just a feeling. All you have to do is be ready to hear what it has to say. Listen and follow it. It will not lead you amiss.

When you finally regain your power of intuition, you will see that you can improve your feminine energy.

Take Things Slowly.

I understand you are in a hurry to regain and improve your feminine energy, but you must know that rushing things will only make your trip on your shoelaces. Boosting your feminine energy is a gradual process that takes time to manifest because it allows time and space for things to unfold slowly.

Be at Peace With Yourself.

To boost your energy, you must be at peace with yourself. Do not set a standard so high that you can't reach it. Stay away from perfectionism, do your best and leave the rest.

Practice patience. This is very crucial. A lot of you do not have patience for yourself and others.

When I was in my early teens, I used to deal a lot with patience. I was the most impatient person anyone had ever met. I nearly put my younger brother in the ER because of my impatience. My parents were out of town for a while and in my hands was the responsibility of being in charge of the family. I had two younger sisters and an immediate younger brother. I divided the chores among everyone. While I played mommy and daddy roles, someone else had to clean the house and mow the lawn. I assigned my brother the mowing the property, and he put it off for three days! The yard still hadn't been done on the day my parents were to return! I was furious.

I didn't want my hypothetical white dress to be stained with dirt from my brother's lack of responsibility. If the lawn wasn't done before my parents returned. I was the one who was going to be in trouble. Looking back now, I was the older one, and I should have known better, but I was in a rage. The rage was a fruit borne out of my impatience.

My brother was standing on the stairs when I punched him in the face, but the little devil held my shirt, and we both went tumbling down the stairs. He blanked out immediately, and I thought he was dead! Luckily for my hypothetical white dress, he came back around a few moments later.

To cut the long story short, I was grounded for the rest of my life!

Impatience takes you nowhere. It is the seed of a whole lot of other nasty stuff. You plant impatience in your heart, which bears the fruits of anger, hot temper, hate, irrational thinking, e.t.c.

To be at peace with yourself, you must start forgiving yourself for your past mistakes. It took me a while to forgive myself for what I did to my brother. Every day, I feared what might have happened if he had gotten seriously injured or, worse, died!

You have to forgive yourself for the sins you've committed. Understand that you did them out of a place of childishness, ignorance, and whatnot. You know better now, and if you had known back then as much as you understand now, you would not have dared to try them.

Forgive yourself. Release yourself from the mental prison you have sentenced yourself to. Free yourself. Be at peace with yourself, and you will see how well you will improve and get better with your feminine energy.

Be unapologetic about what you love doing.

As long as you're not harming yourself and anyone else, be unashamed of what you love doing! When you do the things you love, you become happier, and when you're so glad, there's a high chance for your feminine energy to blossom like a flower in springtime. Do you love reading gory books? Marathons sex?

Volunteering for selfless causes? Going on vacation? What exactly is that thing that sets your soul on fire? Do it freely without shame or guilt. Your feminine energy does not applaud pretense. It wants to know the real you, not the facade you've put up to get people to like you. Be yourself and be it while doing what you love.

Join a support group that is particular to you.

What better way to boost your feminine energy than when you are surrounded by people who are also on the same journey as you? You could go online if you cannot find such a group around you. There are a lot of support groups for different causes online, and what's important is that you become a part of something. Joining a group where you can share your progress, ask, and even answer questions. A group of like-minded people communing together for a common purpose. Doesn't the thought of that make you happy?

If you haven't thought of joining a group, then it's not too late. I remember when I first realized that I might have ADHD. It wasn't noticed early in me as a child because ADHD in girls and boys manifests differently, and it is easier to discover it in male children than in females. I came from a highly religious family. So, no child of my father was permitted to have brain disorders.

I grew up wondering why I was so forgetful and disorganized, basically all the symptoms of ADHD. My friends were utterly normal with neurotypical brains and were thriving in school while I was suffering with my neurodivergent brain.

After it dawned on me that I may have ADHD, I spoke with a friend about my fears, and he advised me to join a support group. I asked how and he said, 'Facebook.' And so, I joined a dozen Facebook pages and groups, and it was one of the best decisions I took. I met many people who were just as confused as I was and others who had it all figured out and ready to help. I felt safe in those groups and could share my story with those who understood me.

Being a part of a supportive group is one of the best decisions you can make. You have got to put this book down right now and get on the internet to look for support groups for women embracing their feminine energy.

MORPHING INTO YOUR BEST SELF

Morphing means transforming, and it means to change, to switch. I have helped many women transform into their best selves, and I am proud of it. It is my life goal to help women become better versions of themselves.

Circumstances of life may have robbed you of the ability to be your best self, your true self, but since you're taking charge of your life now, you're about to dive in and snatch that ability back. It is not too late to do it. I believe in you, and you should believe in yourself too.

When you look in the mirror, who do you see? Do you see your current self or the future version of yourself? Are you interested I'm bringing the future to the present? Do you know who wants to begin that journey today? I think I can hear a 'Yes!'
Well, then, let's get to it.

How to be Your Best Self

Indeed, you need to know how to be your best self before transforming into your best self.

Becoming your best self involves making a conscious effort to ensure that all the areas of your life work together in synergy. You will not become your best self over the night; it will take a series of daily actions to give you the desired results. This journey has its bumps, but with discipline, you will reach the end of the road.

Below are some practical tips that can help you be your best self.

Leave your Comfort Zone.

I think I went too easy on this point. Flee from your comfort zone would have been a better fix but let's get on with this. Your comfort zone is where you feel most at peace and ease, but it's a trap. It's a trap because once you get comfortable in that zone, you lose your life – hypothetically, that is.

The life you've always wanted will not happen to you if you do not leave your comfort zone. Do you want to be a famous fashion designer? Restricting yourself from making mind-blowing designs because you're scared that criticism will take you nowhere! You have to showcase your talent. People who have made history today did not do it while sitting in their comfort zone. It would help if you had a little discomfort to wake up, the comfort zone does not offer that, and that is why you must step out of it now.

It would help if you were brave and fierce in your comfort zone. It may not be easy, but it will be worth it.

To make things more straightforward, here's a list of activities that may help you get out of your comfort zone in no particular order.

Change your Daily Routine.

If you used to wake up by 7 am every morning, change that. Wake up by 6 am. Altering the current rhythm of your life that you are accustomed to will help you move out of your comfort zone faster than you can imagine.

- Learn something new
- Travel to new places
- Learn a new skill
- Practice speaking up

- Meet new people
- Grab opportunities by the horn
- Face your biggest fear
- Practice honesty
- Get comfortable with discomfort
- Make it a habit to always try something new

Focus on Healthy Habits.

This could include eating healthy, exercising, meditating, yoga, e.t.c. Anything that would promote your physical, mental, and emotional well-being. The better version of yourself has to be healthy and fit, and it is up to you to make that happen. You cannot be a better version of yourself if you are unhealthy. Take out time to make a wellness routine for yourself. Starting a healthy habit is one thing, whereas maintaining it is another. You have to be consistent because consistency is key.

Manage Your Time.

I used to suck at managing my time. I got involved in many activities in high school but never learned how to manage my time. This made me always exhausted, and it was almost as though I was doing an 8-5 job while I was just in high school. Good thing I learned how to manage my time later in life before it is too late.

There is nothing to be ashamed of if you don't know how to manage your time. There's always room to learn.

Effectively managing your time will go a long way to impact your achievements in life. You cannot be your best self if you cannot control the time you have on your hands.

Time management separates successful people from the rest, separating a woman who wants to embrace her feminine energy from one who is shying away from it.

How to Manage Your Time:
- Make a to-do list every day
- Set reminders for your tasks
- Give each task a time limit
- Get a planner
- Stick to a routine
- Insist that others respect your time
- Avoid multitasking
- Always plan ahead

Motivate Yourself.
Motivation keeps you going and helps you maintain your stand until you achieve your desired goal. Without motivation, you will have no desire to work hard. Motivation is the driving force that helps achievers accomplish their goals.

I quickly lose my motivation; one thing I use to keep myself on track is bribing myself to a reward. It helps me stay focused because I have something to look forward to.

If the reward system doesn't work for you, you could try the following:

Reminding yourself why you want to do something

If you ate working to save money towards getting a car and you find yourself feeling unmotivated to work, reminding yourself why you're doing what you're doing in the first place will help you. You can put up a photograph of the car or whatever it is you're working on in your room or a place where you can see it every day. That way, your sub consciousness is continually reminded of the goal you are trying to achieve. It is going to be difficult for you to feel unmotivated this way. The same thing goes for when you want to embrace your feminine energy. After meticulously following all the tips and steps provided and still feeling unmotivated, you have to remind yourself why you started in the first place.

- Breaking down your activities into smaller chunks and making them exciting

- Finding yourself an accountability partner. This is someone that is going to hold you accountable for your tasks. They will check on you occasionally to see how you're going with your goals.

- Not running away when it becomes too overwhelming.

- Not being hard on yourself.

At the end of the day, when you're not motivated, you cannot achieve your goals, and when you do not achieve your goals, you automatically are far from being the better version of yourself.

Always Tell the Truth.
This is the same as being honest about everything and letting people know you can be trusted and that they can count on you. You cannot be your best self when you are a lying cheat. The feminine energy is the polar opposite of bad traits. So, if you want to embrace your feminine energy or become your best self, you have to make it a habit to be a truthful and honest person.

Control and Clean Your Mind.
Your mind is powerful and, if left unchecked and uncontrolled, could wreak a lot of havoc. I once met a lady who had lost absolute control over her mind. However, she wasn't even a crack-head. She was just a lady who had lost the ability to be in control of her thoughts. Some studies have been carried out that prove that we are always in our heads half the time.

And that half the time, we are not focused on the outside world. This is such a piece of vital information that needs to be taken seriously. Since we are always in our head almost half the time, we have to clean it thoroughly and make it sparkling clean like you would clean your house. What happens when you live in a filthy house? You get sick. The same thing happens when your mind is dirty.

Avoid Gossiping.
It is a wonder that I haven't talked about this yet, but since we're here now, let's dive into it. If you're gossiping for personal gain, then you've got some backtracking. There are different types of gossip.

While casually talking about someone in their absence may not be too bad, hateful gossip, however, is a terrible thing, and you should make efforts to curb it from your life before you begin reading the next tip.

You cannot be your best self when you are proficient in bringing others down with your mouth. I do not know the image of your best self in your head, but I'm confident it does not involve being vile and uncouth.

Embrace Courtesy.
Remember the five three words? Please, Sorry, Thank you. These words do not just end with our five-year-old self in kindergarten. There are grown women who do not know how to be courteous. They have no atom of goodness in them. Wanting to be your best self means that you will have to be kind and appreciative to people. When you're grateful, say thank you. When you're sorry, say you're sorry. When you want to ask for a favor, say please. It is never too late for you to begin trying. Your mind is your only limit as long as you are thirsty for change.

Take Up New Challenges.
This means that you've stepped out of your comfort zone, set up new goals, and are ready to achieve them. The

challenge you will take on will test you on many levels, which is why it's called a challenge. The beauty of a challenge is that it opens you up to new possibilities. Every day is already a challenge, so do well to take it on.

HOW TO TRANSFORM INTO YOUR BEST SELF

At age 25, I was lost, confused, and unsure of my life's direction. As a child, I got compliments from strangers, telling me I would be a great person growing up. At 25, I figured I was grown enough for those prophecies to begin manifesting, but it didn't seem likely to happen. I became depressed, and my anxiety shot off the roof. Everyone around me tried encouraging me. They said, "You're still young, and you still have your whole life ahead of you."

I didn't know what to hear about their pity party. I was out looking for success, and if I wasn't going to get it in my 20s, then I didn't even want it anymore. Oh, how I look back at those days and shake my head at my ignorance. I am thankful for the time. You see, time always tells. At the end of it all, time will tell.

I went to bed one night feeling extraordinarily disappointed and useless. I lay crying when a light turned on in my head. I had an idea come to me. It was as clear as day, and although it lasted less than a second, I got a clear picture of what I needed to do to stop feeling shitty all the time. I was going to take charge of my life. I had had bursts of emotions like that before in my life. Episodes when I decided to reinvent myself and start new routines, but they never lasted for more than weeks. I always went back to default, but this time around, I was almost sure it would be life-changing. I was going to reinvent myself, and it would last a lifetime. So, I picked up my pen and diary and began jotting down the things I needed to do: habits that I wanted to drop and the new ones I wanted to take on. I was excited about this recent change. It took me about two hours before I rounded up. I had mapped out my life in the diary. It was a lot, but I was convinced it would work out for me.

That was how my life changed. On a lonely night, as I lay crying in bed. Your moment of complete transformation may be different. Of course, it will be different. Yours could come as you read this book. (I hope it does!) But when it comes, endeavor to embrace it.

You must trust the process to transform into your best self. I trusted the process, which was why I got a good result.

You have to trust the flow of time. Good things take time to happen, and I don't know why. It may be because it is destined to last, so it has to take time. Just as gold has to be tried in the fire? Trust that everything makes sense in the end. You are not permitted to give up after the 100th trial and must keep trying until you get it right.

Make room for your feminine side to show. Give it time to blossom. You cannot continue to keep your feminine energy in the closet, and you can make it work side by side with your masculine power and, with time, allow it to override your masculine energy.

Work on your personal development and your self-improvement. Work on a strategy, and have a plan. Do not live life as it comes. Be intentional about your life and make precise decisions to make it work.

Speak to yourself, practice self-dialogue, and ensure you're saying the right things. To create the best version of yourself, you have to be conscious of the things you say to yourself. Be positive and encouraging. Instead of saying, 'I'm a mess,' say, 'I'm a work in progress.' Whenever negative thoughts come up, block them out and replace them with good ones.

Be your biggest cheerleader. Your biggest believer. It took a while before I hacked this. I used to constantly bash myself in my head and internally downgrade myself for being stupid or clumsy whenever I made a mistake. It reached a point when I didn't have a single good thought about myself. It was all wrong. As time went on, it began to affect my life physically. When I had had enough and wanted to drop the bad habit, I found it difficult because it had become second nature. It took visiting my therapist before I could rid myself of the self-destructive habit.

In conclusion, transitioning or morphing into your best self is a very accomplishable goal to make for yourself. You are never too damaged or too broken to be the better version of yourself, to embrace your feminine energy. You, my dear, are not a lost cause.

CHAPTER SEVEN

ENERGY VAMPIRES

"An energy vampire can never 'steal' energy from us unless we consciously or unconsciously permit them to."
- Mateo Sol.

Simply put, an energy vampire is anyone who will drain your emotional energy leaving you feeling depleted. Some people will leave you completely burnt out after conversing with them, and you will feel emotionally drained and exhausted. When this happens, you have every cause to believe that you have just met up with a vampire! Notice how when you have conversations with some people, they leave you feeling all warm, happy, and content on the inside? Such that you do not even want them to go? Well, energy vampires are the total opposite.

Tragic right? Especially when the only type of energy you need is the one that starts with an F. The Feminine Energy.

The only difference between energy vampires and actual vampires is that they are real and can be found everywhere. Energy vampires are toxic and come in whatever gender on the surface of this earth.

They mainly prey on sensitive, emotional, kind, and happy people. It only makes sense that they do because they are trying to suck out all the joy and happiness they miss in their lives from other people. The worst kinds of energy vampires are the ones who are utterly oblivious to the damage they do because they are unaware of the type of energy they possess, which makes it hard to get rid of.

There are multiple ways to combat these joy-sapping individuals. The internet is rich with materials on this topic. Everyone has probably heard the term before. It is okay if you haven't. You probably didn't know they had an actual name, but now that you do, I think it only makes sense that we jump right into the following:

- Types of Energy Vampire
- How to Spot an Energy Vampire
- How to Deal with Energy Vampires
- How to Manage Energy Vampires
- How Energy Vampires Affect Your Feminine Energy
- What to do if You're The Energy Vampire

TYPES OF ENERGY VAMPIRES

Various types of energy vampires drain you in unique ways.

The Gaslighting Vampire

Gaslighting is a form of psychological abuse whereby people question their memory, sanity, and perspective of how certain things occur.

Few things in life are worse than being around a Gaslighting Vampire. People who gaslight would belittle you and your feelings, thereby causing you to question your emotions and if they are valid. For example, whenever you feel violated by them, they would accuse you of being oversensitive even when the situation is life-threatening. They would always accuse you of playing the victim card.

They are often skilled professionals in this profession, and I say this because they are good at what they do. They are good at being horrible people, and if you stick around them, you will be too drained to embrace your authentic feminine energy.

The Clueless Vampire

I classify this group of vampires as 'clueless' because they are unaware of their vampirism. They are often oblivious to the kind of damage that they inflict on people around them.

These vampires come in different forms but primarily manifest as adult babies (i.e., people who have refused to grow up). They go around unleashing their baggage on others because they are too scared to deal with their shit. They are codependent. Helping such people can leave you feeling drained and worn out because you will get too preoccupied attending to their needs, thereby forgetting about yours.

The Narcissist Vampire

These lots cannot show love and compassion and lack the intellect to care about the emotional needs of others. They are self-centered, arrogant, and egoistic. Narcissists will always want to be put first before anyone else but can never return the energy when it is necessary.

They require constant admiration and praise from everyone around them, and when you fail to give them the flowers they do not deserve, they would flip on you and show you a part of them that you never knew existed.

They are charming, two-faced individuals one should never be unfortunate to meet.

The Control Vampire

These lots derive pleasure in treating you like a puppet. They will control your every move. Who you talk to, who you are friends with, what you eat, what you wear. They want to be in charge at all times. This kind of vampire reminded me of my parents when I was a teen. They both wanted me to live my life the way they wanted. Because I was still young and timid, I never had the chance to stand up to them. I often had to quit hobbies and activities I loved so much because they didn't like them. They sucked my energy out until I moved out of their home.

It takes discipline and a thorny heart to handle a controlled vampire. They tend to become aggressive when they feel threatened by rebellion.

The Annoying Vampire

They will make a big deal out of everything and are experts at blowing things out of proportion. Annoying vampires can look cute initially, but as time goes on, you will begin to notice how easily they can drain your energy when you are around them.

Their nagging will give you a headache and a drained spirit. I also like to classify annoying vampires as gossipers. They will say anything about anybody at the slightest provocation, and your secrets are unsafe.

HOW TO SPOT AN ENERGY VAMPIRE

There are different ways to spot an energy vampire, seeing that there are other energy vampires.

They Lack Boundaries

Energy vampires have no concept whatsoever of the word boundaries. They will be all up in your space whenever and however they deem fit. They always have intrusive thoughts and do things without first having a plan. They can decide right in the middle of a conversation that they want to take your car out and drive in the snow for a while. They would not take a no for an answer.

They are Gossipers

Sometimes, gossiping can be harmless, but an energy vampire takes it to a new level. They would want to dissect everyone that has crossed them with a knife and fork while they feed on all the knowledge they know about their victim, and it will be at the cost of your sanity because you will be forced to listen even though it makes you uncomfortable.

They Have The Me-First-Mentality

Putting yourself first in certain situations is an admirable act that needs to be emulated. Still, energy vampires always want to come first in all the scenarios one can think of, even if it means other people would suffer. For example, a disabled person must get on the bus with only one seat left. An energy vampire, having no empathy, will take up the last space because they didn't want to be ten minutes late to a Karaoke night.

They Are Unkind

Some energy vampires are mean, self-centered, and inconsiderate toward the feelings of others. They will step on anyone and walk away without feeling guilty. They are never sorry for their wrongdoings and always claim to be correct.

They are Guilt Trippers

They would guilt trip you into right about anything. They are also excellent at giving an ultimatum. "I won't speak to you again if you don't lend me your hoodie." They are constantly filling you in on the consequences if you do not fulfill their desires.

They Use Everything as an Excuse

Energy vampires will use anything as an excuse to get out of difficult situations. They would blame their shortcomings on their mental illnesses and anything else that serves as a good excuse.

They are Users

Have you ever been used by someone you trusted? For most people, the answer is Yes. Energy vampires are users. They will use you for everything and stay by themselves for what you can do for them and not what they can do for you. If you are compassionate and kind, you are easy prey for them, and they will take advantage of you without batting an eye.

They Always Desire to be the Center of Attention

Energy vampires can be attention seekers. They like the spotlight to always be on them and would not hesitate to bring down heaven and earth if the spotlight is taken away for even a minute.

They will talk over you in conversation and try to come up with a more exciting story just so the attention is focused on them. They do not even care if everyone at the table is bored out of their minds because of them. They see no one else, only themselves.

HOW TO DEAL WITH ENERGY VAMPIRES

Dealing with vampires can be tricky sometimes. Most times, when you try to correct them and set your boundaries with them, you end up being tagged the villain. It can be a dreadful and even more energy-draining experience, so I have curated a few ways to deal with energy vampires.

Limit Contact

Once you have noticed that a person is an energy vampire, reducing contact is wise. Limit contact with them as much as possible. Please do not put yourself in a situation where they can get a hold of you. You have to make yourself less available and then make up your mind to hang out with them less.

Remember that protecting your energy is paramount to your growth; therefore, you shouldn't feel bad about it, so you must put all your sentiments at bay.

Cut them off

I know this may sound pretty drastic, but when a person threatens your mental health and energy, you really should have no mercy for them.

You cannot always be compatible with everyone. Sometimes, we make the mistake of jumping into friendships and relationships with people we think are all "it" because they gave off the right vibe on the first day.

You have power over your life, and it is up to you to choose who you want to stay with and who you want to leave. As Sebastien Richard said, "Life chooses your acquaintance, but you must choose your friends."

Be Aware of Your Strengths

Energy vampires are drawn to you because of your particular strength. An energy vampire does not just go after anybody, and they have specific qualities that make them attracted to you.

These strengths could be that you're kind, a listener, robust and intelligent, e.t.c. and they want to sap away all that quality for themselves.

You can use your strength to leverage them. Work on these strengths and harness them to the fullest. Your muscles are supposed to help you fight your most brutal battle and not allow the enemy to win their fight with you.

Set Boundaries

Boundaries can be challenging to set sometimes, but when you aim to control how much a vampire affects your energy, you just have to do it. I remember having a friend in high school who was a vampire, and we were both roughly fifteen years of age, but she always drained the hell out of me, proving that vampires can come in different ages.

My friend at that time was vulgar and self-centered. She wasn't stable as well. One minute she was funny, kind, and a force to reckon with, and then the next, she was vile, wicked, and could make you tear up in a matter of minutes. It wasn't healthy. I was young and didn't know exactly what to do about the situation.

Avoiding her was my first option, but it was difficult to do so when she was always in my business. Setting boundaries means being direct and firm in your communications. Do not give people the idea that you are okay with being disrespected. Let them understand that there is an extent to which they can joke with you before things start getting momentous.

Learn To Say No

Some people find it very hard to say no, so they are easy prey for energy vampires. Your inability to say no is what energy vampires will feed on. When you cannot reject certain offers and treatments from them, you are automatically made their puppy- always there for their every beck and call.

These two simple letters, 'NO,' can go a long way to protect your energy from vampires. If only you can learn how to use it, then the sky will be your only limit.

The time has come for you to stand up for yourself and do the needful. Put your fears at bay. Remember that you must first face your fears to embrace your feminine energy.

HOW TO MANAGE ENERGY VAMPIRES

There's a vast difference between handling an energy vampire and managing one. Where the former means to put them in their place, the latter means to contain them.

Here's a list of ways you can manage energy vampires.

You Can't Change an Energy Vampire

The first step to managing an energy vampire is understanding that you can't change them or anyone. People will change if they wish to, and nothing you say or do can make them do otherwise.

An old saying goes, *"Change begins with you."*

The best thing you can do is change yourself because change begins with you. You must change your attitudes, character, behaviors, and response to situations. You are in charge of your emotions when you have changed how you react to situations. Your energy becomes secure, leaving the vampires without access to your mind.

Control Your Energy Distribution

Back in my hometown, I had a neighbor who always made me uncomfortable when I was a teen. She was a lot older than I was, and she always succeeded in evoking destructive emotions in me. Since I was small, fragile, and timid, it was easy for her to do those things. Sometimes, she would walk up to me in my front yard whenever I was playing and then tease me until I got angry and started screaming at her.

It was almost a regular pattern. She would come to my yard and tease me, and I would react crazily. Soon enough, I began dreading going out to the yard to play, and eventually, I stopped playing outside together. Thinking back now, I think I handled it pretty well. Sometimes, we don't always have to fight back, and we don't always have to try to prove that we're untouchable.

As a kid, I decided to control my energy distribution even though it meant abandoning my favorite playing spot.

Controlling your energy distribution means getting out of places and situations that would cause you to expel them in the first place, and sometimes, they may be your favorite places, but you have to understand that nothing good comes easy. Protecting and stepping into your energy is what truly matters.

Be Reminded of your Worth

A person who knows their worth does not wallow in the mud with pigs. Knowing your worth means, you will not stoop to the level of energy vampires. When they try to come at you, you look at them and say, "Not today, Satan!"

Work on ways to elevate your self-worth. Invest in upgrading your self-worth. An energy vampire has no business with someone who knows her worth. Knowing your worth helps you effectively manage the vampires.

In addition, knowing your worth and constantly reminding yourself of your worth go hand in hand. You can know your worth but forget it in the whirlwind. Do not let that person be you. Know your worth! Be reminded of your worth!

Know Your Energy Limits

A five-liter water bottle cannot contain six liters of water no matter how hard you try because it was designed only to carry five liters. Likewise, you, as a person, cannot go above your energy limit. This does not in any way imply that there is no room for improvement in your energy limits in a situation that is too low.

Knowing what you can allow in a fight and what you cannot is knowing your energy limits. Making them know that you do not make jokes about your height, body, color, or even your face is one way to make them know your limits.

When you know your limits, you become more conscious and aware of how it is used. You also become particular about who you spend your energy on, and it'll most likely not be on vampires.

Lower Your Expectations

Stop expecting or requiring too much from energy vampires. You will always end up disappointing yourself.

To safely manage them while protecting your energy, you must learn not to put your faith in them. Expect the worst even that way. When the worst happens, you're not surprised because you saw it coming. They are liable to do you dirty and go free without any consequences.

I wish I had known this earlier in life. I always used to expect so much from my parents, who kept letting me down each time. Every time they would make snide comments about most projects I was working on, I would hide in a corner and cry my heart out. "They're my parents; why do they treat me like shit?" This was the rhetorical question I always asked, but as time passed, I began to lower my expectations, and it saved me from many future heartaches.

In conclusion, managing energy vampires may seem a bit extreme, but their actions towards non-energy vampires are not all that fun either.

HOW ENERGY VAMPIRES AFFECT YOUR FEMININE ENERGY

Energy vampires ask for so much from the people around them. Attention, a listening ear, a supporter, etc. They will hijack you to perform all these for them, which may leave you depressed, anxious, and under severe stress.

It is not so fun when you have to baby seat an energy vampire- look after them because they can't do so for themselves. Often, in trying to help these vampires, we turn ourselves into their assistants and abandon our cause to them. They will feed on you because you have given them access to your life.

Energy vampires are manipulators. They sap from your kind heart and make you feel bad for not giving them enough of yourself to feed on. They are psychopaths and sociopaths.

Spending too much time around energy vampires is almost like setting yourself up for suicide, and I agree that most people energy vampires are people you can't avoid. For example, your parents, spouse, or employer. This gives you chronic stress, which can lead to deadly ailments. So much for being a vampire's assistant. Total avoidance of people with such vampire energy is one way to start. You could have an honest conversation with them if they're your spouse.

Remember that you have no excuses to maximize your life and that even in the worst-case scenario, you can emerge a winner if you are deliberate about the winner.

Your feminine energy should always come first. Feed it, nurture it, water it, and watch it blossom. Energy vampires can make it challenging to step into your desired energy. Since you are conditioned to spending your time around them, you will see that you have little to no time for yourself.

Feminine energy, as I have discussed before, is an inherent nature that causes her to behave in a way that screams "naturalness."

When you devote your energy and time to vampires, that's not natural, and that's fake and shouldn't be happening anywhere on God's green earth. Your feminine energy is allergic to unhealthy patterns and behaviors, and serving a vampire is unhealthy and unnatural.

If you have been on the journey of embracing your feminine energy and, at the same time, you have an unhealthy relationship with energy vampires, you are bound to get into a crash halfway through your journey.

How can you pamper yourself the way your femininity requires when all you can think of is the burden placed on your shoulders by these energy vampires? You are bound to lack focus and direction.

Your feminine energy requires you to be relaxed at all times, but the vampires make you stressed out.
Your feminine energy wants you to practice self-love, but the energy vampire wants all that love for himself.

Your feminine energy wants you to know your self-worth, but the energy vampire knows that once you realize that, then no more baby treatments for him. So, he makes you feel worthless.

The energy vampires around you threaten you to embrace your feminine energy, which affects it in all plausible ways, and you have to fight hard against them.

WHAT TO DO IF YOU ARE THE ENERGY VAMPIRE

Energy vampires are not ghosts. They are among us. They are you and me. If you think about it, we have all been energy vampires at some point in our lives, just that it wasn't all on the same frequency.

You tend to be an energy vampire if you have been emotionally wounded. Of course, there are countless reasons why a person would end up as an energy vampire, but they are all just excuses for being a shitty person. Just because you've had a bad run with life does not mean you should make others have a terrible run.

Anyway, if you have read from the beginning of this chapter to this point, you may have noticed that some of the traits of an energy vampire are peculiar to you. Freight not. Many people have discovered more horrendous things about themselves in much more dire conditions. Be thankful that you found it in a book.

There is hope for you to be redeemed, my friend. As I mentioned, you cannot change a person if they do not want to change. Likewise, I cannot change you from being an energy vampire to the best version of yourself if you are not up for the ride. But I have faith in you and that you are willing to change.

Desire To Change

There is no smoke without fire. You have first to desire to make a change before it happens. A passion for change will boost the process and make you see results in no time. A sincere desire to change is the first start.

Look Inwardly For Internal Injuries that Haven't Healed Yet

As I mentioned, most people have injuries that haven't healed yet. It could be from trauma, abuse, or anything. You have been looking past it for too long, and it has gone rotten. To stop being an energy vampire, you have to come face to face with that injury. You have to face it. Look it in the eyes and decide to get over it. This can be extremely difficult because you may not want to be reminded of all the shit you have gone through, but the only way to become a better person is to heal from within.

Ask Questions and Listen to Answers

Since being an energy vampire has become like second nature to you, you may not know how to treat people right anymore. This is the part where you begin to ask questions. It could be your co-worker, your friends, or your spouse. Anyone that you interact with a lot. Ask them questions about how you treat them, how your actions affect them, and what you can do to improve. When they respond, listen. If possible, take a pen and paper or, better still, record the conversation on your phone.

Ask for Forgiveness / Forgive Yourself

Asking for forgiveness is a sure way to get all the guilt from your back. You may have made people feel terrible about themselves in the past. Now is the time to seek their forgiveness, for your conscience's sake.

Having the desire to change means being willing to take on humility. The people you ask forgiveness from may not accept it. They may even hate you more, but what's important is that you do your part and leave the rest.

As you ask for forgiveness from others, also ensure that you forgive yourself. Do not shame yourself for the horrible person that you once were.
Remember that you are a strong woman and are capable of forgiving yourself.

CHAPTER EIGHT

SELF-AWARENESS

"Knowing yourself is life's eternal homework"- Felicia Day.

I was going in and out of many relationships in my early 20s. They never lasted more than three months, no matter how serious I wanted them to be. I took corrections from the people I was dating badly. I didn't want to learn or own up to my mistakes, and I couldn't accept them or learn from the mistakes I had made. It is safe to say that I lacked emotional maturity, a side effect of lacking self-awareness.

Self-awareness is the bedrock of emotional intelligence. It is the acceptance of one's individuality and the ability to examine ourselves without bias. It helps you see and better understand your shortcoming, talents and gifts, personality, and potential.

To fully understand the concept of Self-awareness, we have to take a brief look at the following:

- Types of Self-Awareness
- Benefits of Self-Awareness
- Barriers To Self-Awareness
- Signs of Low Self Awareness
- How to improve your Self-Awareness
- How self-awareness boosts your Feminine Energy

By the time you are at the end of this chapter, you will have obtained a definitive insight into self-awareness and be equipped to fully harness its powers.

TYPES OF SELF-AWARENESS

There are two significant types of self-awareness. The **Public (external)** and **Private (internal)** self-awareness.

Public/External Self-Awareness

Public self-awareness focuses on people's understanding of how others view or perceive them. It can be either positive or negative, but what's important here is that you're aware of their perspective. When a person is self-aware externally, they genuinely realize their importance in the life of others and can act accordingly.

Public self-awareness helps you understand what people think of you and whether your actions are welcomed or rejected/if they are happy or not with you.

When a person can judge from the point of external self-awareness, they are looking at themselves from the perspective of others, thereby improving their behavior and attitude to certain conditions.

Private/Internal Self-Awareness

This is being aware of something about yourself that others may not be aware of. It focuses on your inner values, thoughts, goals and aspirations, weaknesses and strengths, and how you see them.

Knowing that your current job as a secretary does not match your true passion for being a chef means that you are aware of your true passion and not just floating through life.

Self-aware people can manage and control their feelings because they know what bothers them.

BENEFITS OF SELF-AWARENESS

It Frees us From Being Biased
Biases can either be conscious or unconscious.

Conscious Bias
This is a type of bias you are aware of. It happens consciously, and you can act on it with intent.

Unconscious Bias
These are stereotypes or beliefs that operate outside a person's awareness.

They influence the way we interact with the world at large. Being self-aware helps us to confront our biases and eventually let go of them. Confronting our biases through self-awareness allows us to learn, drop old habits and grow. We are given the ability to be acquainted with people who are open-minded and free of bias.

It Helps Improve Our Skills
Self-awareness helps us better our skills by recognizing our capabilities and strengths. A self-aware person will focus on improving their abilities and do what they have to improve.

When we are self-aware, we can distinguish between what we know we will do for the long term and what is casual because we are so aware of our emotions and feelings that we know what we want.

I didn't have a niche specific to me in the fast. I used to write about everything from different genres, and this was because I wasn't self-aware enough to know what I truly wanted to write about. That lack of self-awareness hindered me from picking a specific niche and working on it. The same applies to all kinds of skills when you are not self-aware.

It Helps to Build Better Relationships
Self-awareness heightens the happiness within yourself, which is an essential ingredient for developing strong and meaningful relationships with people.

People with solid self-awareness experience longer and happier relationships than those without.

Self-awareness allows you to be familiar with specific patterns and behaviors that are bad news. When you're self-aware, you will instinctively know and recognize them and save the stress of repeatedly making the same mistakes.

Lastly, when you are self-aware, you become more in tune with the thoughts and feelings of others. You can treat them better, which will eventually help your relationship blossom.

It Decreases Stress
Self-awareness can help you manage stress levels by distinguishing your emotions and feelings from who you are as a person and entity.

When you practice self-awareness regularly, you will always feel in control of your emotions, and you will be able to calm yourself whenever you are stressed.

It Increases Happiness
When you're on the quest to discover happiness, a must-have is not a bowl of your favorite meal or a hot man riding a chariot. It's self-awareness!

Since self-awareness lets us embrace and understand our true selves, it directly leads to an unending supply of happiness; how else can you be delighted if you've not accepted who you are?

BARRIER TO SELF-AWARENESS

Various barriers can ultimately hinder you from ever attaining self-awareness, and I will walk you through a few of them. To fully enjoy being self-aware, you must pull down all the obstacles you find on this list.

Fear of Unpleasant Emotions
People are afraid of opening the can of worms they've carried all their lives, forgetting that opening up is a worm that is actually upon the lip.

Unpleasant emotions can erupt when you're trying to be self-aware. There may be certain things about yourself that you do not want to face. You're scared of your reality, your truth forgetting that when you encounter these emotions, you can indeed be free.

You have to get over yourself and be honest with things you do not want to face.

Fear of Revealing Our True Selves
No matter what they say, people would always want to look their best in front of other people. Sure, they may not want to look flawless, but people would rather quietly hide their skeletons in the cupboard and live their lives peacefully. Self-awareness ruins that pattern because you do not want to be perceived as weak.

Revealing those faults, we've worked so hard to hide through self-awareness can be difficult.

That there, my friend is a barrier. We want to be seen as perfect, so we choose not to know ourselves deeply.

Lack of Mindfulness
Mindfulness helps us to recognize what is going on in our minds with each moment that passes without judgment. It deals with introspection. When you are not mindful, you can't be self-aware.

Feeling Uncomfortable When You Focus on Yourself
Most people are scared to put themself first. They have been used to putting everyone else in front of them, so they get scared when it's time to get in front.

It's a pathetic situation, being afraid of bettering yourself.

I would say that this situation is mainly caused when people are the victims of an energy vampire or a plain old narcissist.

They have always been conditioned to take care of other people. Now, they feel like their needs are invalid and do not require any improvement in their lives.

This kind of barrier is hard to break because your heart wants to change and get better, and your mind has been conditioned to believe that you do not require it.

SIGNS OF LOW-SELF AWARENESS

Lacking self-awareness is such a wrong side of the spectrum to be on but at the same time, finding a person who has complete self-awareness of themselves is astoundingly rare.

People can clearly understand themselves, but they may still be unable to tell what they look like to people on the outside. Also, a person can clearly understand what people see them as, but they have no idea what they are themselves on the inside.

Here are ways to know when a person lacks it:

They Are Always on The defensive side
They are steadily defending themselves. They never take corrections, admit they're wrong, and never say sorry. Such a person lacks self-awareness.

They can't be fully trusted.
A person who lacks self-awareness cannot be fully trusted. One is unsure if one can handle tasks and decisions because one does not even know themselves.

They Play the Victim Card
People who lack self-awareness always think they are being oppressed, and thus, they play the victim card.

They Are Very Critical of Others
People who criticize others lack self-awareness, which may imply that they are better than those they criticize. This may give them a heightened sense of importance which isn't pure and accurate because it didn't come from the right source.

They Are Vague About Their Feelings
A person who is vague about their feelings may lack self-awareness, and they cannot talk plainly about their feelings which may look like they're avoiding something. A self-aware person communicates their emotions in clear and understandable terms.

Living in the Past and Worrying About the Future
A person who is not self-aware will always make the mistake of worrying about the future, thinking about the past, and making no effort to work on and appreciate the present.

Always Daydreaming
Daydreaming can be fun sometimes. It even serves as an escape from this world for a short while, but it becomes a problem when someone dwells too much on it. A self-aware person does not spend all their time wishful thinking. Sure, this can be particularly hard for people

who suffer from certain mental illnesses that make them fixated on certain activities for long periods, but this is where the concept of self-awareness comes in. You have to make an effort to be self-aware. No excuses.

Regular Emotional Outbursts
There's no harm in having an outburst from time to time. After all, we are humans and prone to experience unavoidable stress that can make us go crazy occasionally. Still, a person who lacks self-awareness would always have an emotional outburst at the slightest inconvenience. They are clueless about how to handle and control their emotions because they are not self-aware.

HOW TO IMPROVE YOUR SELF-AWARENESS

Improving your self-awareness is the next available step to take. Please do not sleep on it; here's how to do it.

Get out of your comfort zone
Leaving your comfort zone is the first of many things that you can do to improve your self-awareness. Staying in your comfort zone makes you too comfortable to get your life together, and you have to get out there and indulge yourself in new experiences. It allows you to think about how you act in unfamiliar situations.

Your comfort zone allows you to be on auto-pilot. This means that you cannot do pretty much anything new. You will remain stagnant and never have the chance to discover anything new about yourself. You cannot achieve much while on auto-pilot. To improve your self-awareness, you have to leave your comfort zone.

Identify Your Triggers
What is that thing that makes you go crazy, stressed, and jealous whenever it happens? Pounder on it to discover your triggers. When you recognize what triggers negative emotions, you can avoid them in the future. This is what self-awareness is all about—knowing yourself to the fullest and working only with the people and things that bring out the best in you.

Identifying your triggers lets you become more conscious of how you react to them, and at the end of the day, you will become a calm, cool, and collected woman who is entirely in line with her feminine energy.

Let Your Walls Down
Who knows, you may have knowingly or unknowingly built a wall around yourself that keeps people out of your life. It may be a response to a bad thing you were made to go through in the past.

Building walls may also mean shutting things out that we do not like for no reason. I have built a barrier against people who did nothing to me because immediately I wouldn't say I liked it. Also, I have made walls against some aspects of my life that I do not find interesting, and I locked myself out of my own life.

One becomes more self-aware when one learns to put their defenses down and then see themselves in a different light than they are used to before.

Take a Personal Survey From Others About Yourself
It doesn't have to be too formal, and you can curate a few questions and pass them on to your friends and families. We all know that the opinions of others about ourselves

should not matter but in this case, you are only trying to improve yourself and see things from the external point of view.

When the answers to your questions come in, you can look at them and then choose the ones you will work on.

Keep an Open Mind
You are going to hear things that you do not like or that you will argue are untrue. But, you will have to understand their point of view and perspective.

Keeping an open mind will help you get more corrections and also help you adhere to them. A self-aware person also keeps an open mind, and that's how you'll eventually improve yours.

HOW SELF-AWARENESS BOOSTS YOUR FEMININE ENERGY

When I began indulging in the study and act of Feminine Energy, I was lacking a bit on the self-awareness path. Sure, I had a lot of knowledge about self-worth and self-love, but I didn't know about self-awareness. I was still easily triggered by the slightest inconvenience, didn't know how to manage my temper, and was still living life not knowing who I was. My image of myself in my head differed from who I was in the grand scheme of things.

In my head, I was the sweet young lady who loved her pets, looked at things from her perspective, and was equally lovely to deserving people. It wasn't until I came across a video where the topic of self-awareness was being discussed that I had a whole new revelation about myself.

I quickly keyed into the self-awareness plan because I didn't want to be left behind for whatever reason. I began watching videos and reading books that were relevant to self-awareness. I asked questions nicely.

Days turned into weeks, and I was recording a tremendous change in my life. I didn't see things from the same angle I used to before. I was more in control of my emotions than ever before, and I could remove myself from situations that drained my energy and made me all work up.

Subsequently, I blossomed more in my feminine energy, which was noticeable to the people around me. They saw the change! If people don't know the difference, you aren't doing anything yet, honey!

Your self-awareness and feminine energy should go hand in hand, but most importantly, your feminine energy will not fully flourish without you having a sense of self-awareness.

A woman who is in her feminine energy and who also is self-aware is bound to thrive in whatever she puts her mind to. Your self-awareness makes everything more manageable, and you no longer have to stress about irrelevant issues because you already know how to handle them. You can also graciously come out of situations that compromise your energy because you already saw it coming from the onset.

Self-awareness works like magic sometimes. Imagine being able to control your feelings, imagine living a life free of throwing tantrums and constantly complaining about everything.

I'm not saying that joining the bandwagon of self-aware women will shield you from getting hurt or falling victim to circumstances.
But it can minimize the effect those situations will have on you. The sense that others, while other women would throw a tantrum because their car broke down on their way to work, you, on the other hand, will be calm and take care of the situation like a woman in control of her emotions, would.

This is your sign of embracing self-awareness today.

CHAPTER NINE

MEDITATION

"Meditation nourishes the mind in the same way that food nourishes the body." - Anonymous.

Meditation is a practice in which a person or group of people use a unique technique to train the attention and awareness of their minds to achieve a clear, calm state of mind. Meditation is practiced in various religions across the world.

Meditation is a great way to enrich your feminine energy. Since it helps you achieve a clear mind, you can fully harness your potential with your power.

Let's take a look at the following to help us better understand meditation:

- Types of Meditation And Ways to Meditate
- Meditation Benefits
- How Meditation Increases Feminine Energy

TYPES OF MEDITATION AND WAYS TO MEDITATE

An interesting fact worth noting is that there are as many ways to meditate as there are many sports worldwide!

When you look for information online or in magazines, you will see that there are zones of meditation styles to carry out. The different types of meditation equally have other benefits. So, you will have to choose a meditation style that is peculiar to you.

We are going to explore only the most popular types of meditation, and I hope that you will be able to find a meditation technique that will be best for you.

Firstly, meditation has been classified into two parts, namely.

- **Focused Attention**

- **Open Monitoring**

Focused Attention
This is simply focusing your attention on a single object during the meditation session. It may either be tangible or intangible.

The ability to keep your mind focused on a chosen object will make distractions almost non-existent. Doing this will increase the depth of your attention.

Open Monitoring
This is the opposite of focused attention meditation. In this method, one focuses on all aspects of their experience without judgment or bias, and one should be

able to accept their starting thoughts and emotions without judgment.

Now, to the different kinds of Meditation and how to get started with a few of them.

Mindfulness Meditation
It is the type of meditation in which you focus immensely on being aware of what you're seeing and feeling in the moment without interruption.

How To Practice Mindfulness
Take a seat: Take a seat in a calm and serene environment. It could be in your room or backyard so long you aren't going to get any disturbance.

Set a Time Limit: If it's your first time, you can make it short, say, 5-15 minutes.

Take a comfortable Position
You have to stay in a position that is comfortable for you. You can even do it while lying, but if you're prone to falling asleep quickly, then I highly do not recommend that. Just get into any comfy position you are sure you can be in, like 5-15 minutes.

Feel Your Breath
Now, you are going to take notice of your breath. How you inhale and exhale, and do it slowly.

Always Bring Your Mind to the Present
Commonly, your mind may begin to wander. When it

does that, ensure you bring your attention back to your breath.

Be Patient with your Mind
Your mind will wander a lot. Please do not be mad at it. Give it time, and it will soon learn to keep still.

Focused Meditation
This is the method of focusing on something intently as a way of staying in the present to slow your mind down from wandering. It involves concentrating using any of the five senses. It is ideal for anyone who wants to hone their attention and concentration abilities.

How to Practice Mindful Meditation
Choose a place to Meditate: Again, choose a home—a quiet, serene environment where you wouldn't get disturbed.

Choose a target to focus on
It could be anything from feeling your sensation to repeating a mantra.

Sit in a comfortable position
Try to be as comfortable as possible.

Be relaxed
No need for panicking. Be relaxed. You can do this. I am rooting for you.

Shift Your Attention to your focus point constantly
Whenever you feel your mind drifting, always direct it back to your focus point. Center yourself on your target's visual, sound, sensation, smell, or other details. It'll be much easier to stay focused that way.

Keep Practicing

You may not get it right on the first trial, but keep practicing. Meditation can't be learned in one session. Also, increase your time limit as you go so you don't remain dormant. Everything good takes time.

Spiritual Meditation

There are two types of spiritual meditation.

The first one centers on religion and is done with a desire to connect with a higher power or God.

The second is a form of meditation that takes you to the abysses of who you are. It connects you to your spirit and unfolds layers of understanding and beliefs to deduce who you are.

Since we are discussing our feminine energy and how meditations influence it, we will focus mainly on the second.

How to Practice Spiritual Meditation

Choose a comfortable position
I cannot put enough emphasis on this.

Experience the process
 Loosen up and let things take their course. You can be just a spectator who watches on the sideline as things unfold. Allow your mind to penetrate your deepest thoughts.

Accept the Thoughts
As you sit to meditate, no doubt you will be bombarded by thoughts. It is bound to happen. The hard part is that you will not react to them. You will let them come and go, but you will not indulge them.

Reflect on Yourself:
1. Allow your mind to wander back to your breath and surroundings.
2. Be conscious of where you are.
3. Slowly open your eyes and, at the same time, let the effect of the meditation take its course.
4. Acknowledge that something has happened and that you feel better than before you began.

Transcendental Meditation
It was founded by an Indian guru, Maharishi Mahesh Yogi. Transcendental meditation is the technique for detaching oneself from anxiety by repeating a silent mantra in your head, and it is commonly done in a quiet, dimly lit room.

Once upon a time, you could only learn this practice from a trained Transcendental Meditation teacher. Filmmaker David Lynch used a random German word for his mantra instead of paying a licensed TM teacher, and his method proved to be more effective than the ones the TM teachers assigned to people.

Transcendental meditation mantras are not actual words, and they may not even have a meaning, but the key ingredient is in the vibrations they make when they are pronounced.

TM teachers will give you a mantra based on your age and gender. You can find the different sounds for your specific age and gender online.

How to Practice Transcendental Meditation
Set the time. Say 15-20 minutes. Seat in a comfortable chair, keep your back and neck straight and close your eyes.

Be completely still and quiet for a while. At least, 30 seconds.

Relax and let the mantra come to mind. It won't be initially at the forefront of your thoughts, but give it a while. After some time, I slowly make it the main focus of my mind. It won't automatically push the other thoughts. They would fight for your attention but pay no sense to them.

Repeat the mantra with conscious effort. Repeat it only mentally. Your voice is not needed.

When your alarm goes off, remain in that position for at least three minutes, and sit quietly before the world returns to you.

Open your eyes and take a few deep breaths before getting up and going about your day.

Loving-Kindness Meditation
This kind of meditation strengthens feelings of love, kindness, and compassion. Those who practice this technique can increase their capacity for forgiveness, self-acceptance, and connection to others.

Integrating this meditation technique into your routine is essential if you are looking to embrace your feminine energy.

How to Practice Loving-Kindness Meditation

You should know the first step by now, sister! Choose a comfortable position!

Imagine yourself experiencing complete wellness and inner peace. Imagine you feeling perfect love for yourself and accepting all your flaws. Focus on these thoughts. Acknowledge that you are enough for yourself. Slowly begin to breathe in and out. Imagine exhaling tension and stress and living in goodness, wellness, and love for yourself.

Repeat a few phrases that you think connect well with you. E.g., I am beautiful. I am worth it. I am happy.

If your attention drifts, revert to your breathing and focus on it.

Now, shift your focus to your loved ones. Begin to think about how much you love them and are grateful for them. Do it one person at a time, and visualize them as being healthy and at peace with themselves.

When you feel you've done enough, slowly open your eyes and sit still for a few moments as you begin to bask in the euphoric feeling that comes with loving-kindness meditation.

Visualization Meditation

This is simply using guided imagery, ideas, and symbols, to cultivate a sense of mindfulness. It is almost similar to mindfulness meditation.

While on visualization meditation, your focus is on engaging your imagination. It may help to enhance your creativity, achieve motivation and goals, improve your self-image, e.t.c.

How To Practice Visualization Meditation

1. Get into a comfortable position in a serene environment

2. Close your eyes and begin to breathe slowly. Do this until you have a rhythm.

3. Visualize a place where you feel safe, content, and calm. It could be a place you have visited, somewhere you read in a book, or saw in a movie.

This part may be tricky, but use your five senses to connect more to that place. What does it smell like? What does it feel like? Is it hot or cold? Is it raining or sunny?

Imagine yourself moving forward into this visualization. Imagine taking a walk in the area, scenting the roses on the sidewalk, or having a scoop of ice cream from the truck.

Now, breathe slower. Imagine a tranquil feeling radiating around your body. Imagine living in wellness and exhaling tension.

Repeating this process, you can stay in this zone for as long as you want. When you feel ready, you can step out of this vision. Also, remember that you can return to this vision any time you want. Let nothing be a barrier.

Other types of meditation include:

Mantra meditation
Progressive meditation
Movement meditation

BENEFITS OF MEDITATION

The popularity of meditation is rapidly increasing as people are tapping into it daily for its many health and physical well-being benefits.

People are using meditation to relax and cope better with stress. However, the list goes on and on. Here's a list of what motivation does.

Reduces Stress
This is one of the first things that meditation does and why most people who practice meditation today pick it up.

In this crazy little world that we live in, people tend to be stressed out, and mediation is a way to escape it.

Strengthens and Promotes Mental Health
Most meditation techniques can improve the sense of self-image, self-awareness, self-worth, and self-love.

Enhances Peace of Mind
When they ask what they truly want, they'll tell you, "I just want some peace of mind."

Well, I've got some news for you. Meditation gives one a sense of calm and peace. People who meditate can attest to this. I can attest to this. Honestly, you have to take up mediation for a change.

Helps to Lengthen Attention Span
Meditation can help you increase your executive attention, and a little practice every day is a great start. Interestingly, you do not necessarily have to do the most because you begin to see the changes.

Increase Patience and Tolerance
Meditation can transform you from being a hot-headed person to a calm one. Meditation entails self-reflection and self-awareness, which is necessary if you want to be patient and tolerant.

Reduces Anxiety
Meditating is so powerful that it can create a sense of quiet mind, reducing anxiety and helping you get through the day without pressure.

Reduces Memory Loss
For those who experienced age-related memory loss, it's about time you ditch the medications and hop on to a more natural way of doing things. Studies have shown

that despite advanced age in older adults, meditating has helped to give them more impressive mental clarity.

Improves Proper Sleep
Meditating can help you achieve a more pleasant, deep sleep void of disturbance if you struggle with an irregular sleeping pattern. You will be able to live more peacefully.

Can Decrease Blood Pressure
Meditating can decrease blood pressure by putting less strain on your heart and nerves. Blood pressure will drop over meditation and people who regularly do it. This can ultimately reduce heart-related diseases.

In conclusion, meditation will not bring lasting healing to your problems. It is like going to the gym monthly and expecting to get fit; going to the gym is what results. In the same sense, periodically indulging in meditation will give you the ultimate result you want.

An upside to meditating is that everyone can do it, and it can be done in your home or at a meditation center. You can indulge in a wide range of meditation styles, and each has its strength and benefits.

Meditating will ultimately improve your life. What better gift to give yourself than that?

HOW MEDITATION INCREASES FEMININE ENERGY

During the period when I began focusing on learning more about Self-awareness, I began to also dive into meditation. It wasn't new to me because I tried it twice at some point.

When I was a young teen, I tried meditation with a few friends at a sleepover. It was challenging to keep my thoughts from tumbling over one another. The other girls seemed to be getting the hang of it, but I was conflicted. Each time I tried to keep my mind still, my thoughts increased.

"I wonder if I'll get my period tomorrow... I don't think I've got any tampons left. The air smells crazy here. Good thing tomorrow's Saturday. I wonder if mom would let me have my sleepover."

At some point, I gave up and just let my mind wander. At the end of the torturous fifteen minutes, the other girls giggled and talked about how relaxed and at ease they felt.

After that night, I tried it one more time at another sleepover I had with a couple of friends while I was in college. We had just rounded up exams that semester, and all felt burnt out. One of my friends suggested we hang out at her parent's house, a short drive from campus. I always wondered how she coped with going to school every day from her parent's real home.

We managed to sneak a few bottles of champagne into the house without her parent's notice. We stayed up all night in her room while we drank and talked about how the semester had gone. It felt like I was a child again and having one of those little sleepovers. That was the idea, anyone.

"Let's all meditate!" I suggested the Chinese transfer student with whom I wasn't close friends.

Everyone in the group except me agreed instantly. It was undoubtedly beginning to feel like the sleepover I had with my friends as a little girl.

I was tipsy from the champagne, so I just shrugged and joined them. All six twenty-something-year-olds sat on crossed legs on the carpet and began to dig into their inner selves.

"Okay, this isn't so bad," I thought. "Did I return my mom's call? Oh shit, I didn't turn off the light in my dorm before I left. I need to pee. The waiter at the wine shop was cute, and I could have sworn he was checking me out too...."

So, I tried my best to commit to the activity, but I couldn't.

My thoughts were jumbling on one another as the last time I tried. The Chinese transfer student had given us a few tips before we commenced. He was our coach for the session, but even then, I still couldn't get it right. I felt very disappointed in myself.

My journey through embracing my feminine energy brought me to my understanding of self-awareness which in turn brought me to the mighty act of meditating, and ever since then, my life has truly changed.

Meditating is beneficial in vast ways. You can learn to love and appreciate yourself in different ways. Meditation will increase your feminine energy because it makes you more in control of your energy.

Through meditation, you can expel bad energies and vibes and absorb good energy by controlling your thoughts and fixating on only the things you want. Meditating is like getting rid of harmful toxins in your system, and it is worth a try and highly recommended by me.

CHAPTER TEN

BE THE ONE WHO LEAVES WHEN IT BECOMES TOXIC

"No partner in a love relationship should feel that they have to give up an essential part of themselves to make it viable." - May Sarton.

In my final year in college, I had a classmate called Mitchell who was in a toxic relationship with her boyfriend, Ben. She had been with him for seven years, and things were starting to get rocky. She confided in me multiple times, and I gave her the same answer every time.

"Mitchell, leave that man!"

She wouldn't listen to me. They had been together for so long, and she was convinced that Ben was her soulmate. I understood then that it would be difficult for her to leave him, but it was either that or her mental health would continue deteriorating, and everything else would go downhill. Already, she was missing classes and had failed a couple of tests. We were in our final year, so it was a tricky time for one's emotional health to get in the way. Mitchell and her Ben used to be on the same page, but as time passed, it started to seem like they were reading different books entirely.

Ben was schooling at a different college, and before they left for college, he swore they could make a long-distance relationship work. Mitchell had suggested that they both take a break, and if they graduated and saw that they were still attracted to each other, they could continue from where they stopped.

In the end, Mitchell got accustomed to the long-distance relationship. She remained faithful to him for the four years she was at the college; now, with only three months till our finals and graduation, Ben had turned a new leaf. He wasn't as supportive as he used to be in the past. Mitchell returned to the dorm every time they met, feeling mentally drained and exhausted.

She would cry and tell me that he was mean to her, that he snapped at the slightest mistake, and that things weren't as they used to be. The worst part was that Ben always claimed it was all in her head, that he still loved her deeply.

One thing I knew for sure was that there was no smoke without fire. If there were nothing to worry about then, Mitchell wouldn't have constantly complained about how much he had changed.

Ben broke up with her a day before our finals began over a text. Mitchell broke down and had to be admitted to the hospital. She was there for three days and missed a couple of examinations. Thankfully, she was allowed to retake the courses she missed. In the end, Mitchell barely managed to graduate with a good result. Every time I remember her, I am always filled with sadness. No one deserved to go through that, but she was unlucky. This is why you should always be the one to leave first when it becomes toxic.

WHAT IS A TOXIC RELATIONSHIP?

A toxic relationship is an unhealthy relationship where one feels disturbed, drained, misunderstood, trapped, and insignificant. It takes all your energy and confidence away, and toxic relationships are not romantic relationships.

Let us look at the following:

- Types of Toxic Relationships
- Signs of A Toxic Relationship
- Toxic Relationships and Mental Health
- Toxicity In Friendships
- Getting Out of a Toxic Relationship and Getting Over A Toxic Relationship
- How Staying In Toxic Relationships Affects Your Feminine Energy

TYPES OF TOXIC RELATIONSHIPS

There are numerous types of toxic relationships present in our world today, and they can manifest in the most subtle ways. Knowing as many unhealthy relationships as they exist is essential so you can be informed and thoroughly combat them whenever they manifest in your relationships with friends and families.

1. The Controller

If your partner always has an excessive need to always be in charge of controlling your life and decisions and feels like you can't do anything right, then chances are that you may be dealing with a toxic person. You may find yourself constantly compromising to keep the peace.

2. The Table-Tuners

These people like to turn the tables around. They are on the same pedestal as gaslighters. If you have ever tried to tell them that you are unhappy because they offend you, and you somehow find yourself pacifying them because you upset them with your complaints, that is a sign.

You suddenly forget about your initial hurt and carter to theirs because they suddenly play the victim card, and as time goes on, you begin to avoid bringing up their shortcomings because you don't want to upset them. That right there is toxic.

3. Competitive Relationships

A relationship should be a safe space void of competition and rivalry, and a person should be able to relax and not be at war. If your partner is always looking for ways to outdo and compete with every milestone you've achieved, then you have cause to be worried. However, competition can sometimes be healthy, but you can tell when it becomes draining and abnormal. Always remember that you should be partners in love, not war.

4. Trust Issues

Most people deal with trust issues, which can be either mild or severe. When a relationship lacks trust, it can be a brooding house for harmful thoughts, loneliness, jealousy, and constant suspicion. With time, it can lead to emotional and or physical abuse.

5. Double Standard Relationships

Double standards are principles that favor one person over another. Double standards in relationships can bring about bias and inequality. There are lots of ways that it can be manifested. For example, your partner may see nothing wrong with having lots of friends of the same sex but the moment you inform them that you are going to hang with your friends over a couple of drinks, they'll get angry and try to manipulate you into thinking that you're doing something wrong.

Double standards are an ugly phenomenon. What's worse is that your partner can be blind to their double standards. Almost as though everyone can see it except them.

If you experience similar situations, then you may be in a toxic relationship. Double standards in relationships are bad news and should be avoided at all costs.

6. Victim & Predator

The victim in this toxic relationship feels guilty even when they have g done anything wrong. This is because of the passive-aggressive victimization of the predictor. It is usually subtle and is an effective strategy of manipulation that occurs regularly in the relationship. Passive aggressiveness is unseen; it only leaves the victim with sensations.

7. The Pathological Liar

Personally, nothing irks me more than a lair—a pathological liar. Pathological liars will tell compulsive lies that do not benefit them, and when you catch them in the lie and call them out, they will continue to lie and not feel bad about it.

However, there is a difference between a compulsive liar and a pathological liar.

A compulsive liar will lie to feel more significant. Meanwhile, a pathological liar manipulates you with lies to get their way.

Pathological liars will add additional implausible details to their stories even after exposure. You'll end up feeling confused and begin questioning yourself.

8. The Perfectionist

The fact is that you'll never measure up to them. A perfectionist will always see something wrong with you, regardless of your talent and innovation. You won't ever be able to accomplish anything well enough as far as they're concerned.

Spending time with them is always draining because they constantly demand changes from you to meet their requirements.

9. **The Insecure and Jealous One**

They will also be jealous of you, and it's weird because why are they in a relationship with someone they are envious of in the first place? They may frequently accuse you of wanting to leave them after the slightest fight. They lack confidence in themselves and want to take you down with them.

Other types of toxic relationships include:

Aggressive or Abusive Partner, e.t.c

Signs You're In a Toxic Relationship

People close to me used to have power over my emotions. Just one statement from them could have been swimming in agony or shouting for joy.

Almost everyone has that one person who can do and undo their world. It gets very destructive when you have no control over the power that they wield over you. This is where the learning and unlearning process begins. As a woman trying to embrace her feminine energy, you have to get a hold of your emotions. I mean, rip it out of the hands of people holding it hostage.

Signs that you are in a toxic relationship cannot always be easily detected. That's why most people marry poisonous people, and 15 years later, they want to file for a divorce. However, some signs cross the threshold. Naturally, your relationships ought to be a source of joy and happiness, not fear and frustration. When it is the latter, you know what you're up against.

Other signs of a toxic relationship include:

Communication with your partner is non-existent
Do your conversations sound like two strangers on Twitter arguing about a gender-neutral doll? That's not a healthy relationship.

You Feel Uneasy
If you feel uneasy in your guts, you should probably take it seriously and look for more signs. For the umpteenth time, you are supposed to feel safe and at ease in your relationships. Something is wrong if you're getting the opposite of these feelings.

Lack of Support From Your Partner
A mutual desire to see your partner succeed is a significant characteristic of a healthy relationship. When this is missing, you know you have something toxic going on.

Disrespect
Do you notice a lack of regard for boundaries you have set up? Lack of attentiveness?

Physical Violence
It starts with punching the wall and destroying the house furniture because it gets your turn. The right time to run away is when they're doing the walls and furniture.

You Feel Neglected
Is it like you're a child again, and your mom's too busy to look at your homework because she's painting her nails and watching a soap opera? Weirdly specific, I know. You get the idea. Your partner should be able to have time for you and vice versa.

Low Self-Esteem
You can feel your self-esteem slowly slipping away. A healthy relationship will build your self-esteem and make you more confident, not the other way around.

Toxic Relationship And Mental Health

Toxic relationships can cause a lot of damage to our mental and emotional health, and they can also be hard to recover from. This is why evaluating your relationship before going into them is essential. Spend as much time as possible on the talking stage before moving into the relationship.

The quality of your relationship will determine the strength of your mental health. When it is toxic, it will leave you feeling drained and down, give you anxiety & depression, and high-stress levels, and go you walking around with emotional baggage.

Staying in a toxic relationship can land you anywhere from a hospital to a rehabilitation center, showing how much impact it has on us and our mental health. A woman stepping into her feminine energy must put her mental health before anyone, and she should be number one in her book, which is part of self-care.

Toxicity in Friendships

A romantic relationship is not the only kind of relationship that can be toxic. It is also not the only kind of relationship that you should pay attention to.

Toxicity in friendships exists. We like to turn a blind eye to this for fear of losing these people.

Toxic friendships manifest in numerous ways. Some of them include the following:

Dismissing your opinions
Your opinions are never good enough for whatever situation they try to get out for. They will talk you down even before you begin making suggestions.

You Feel Trapped and Obligated to be their friend.
They give you breathing space and are always on your tail, ensuring you never leave them. They pose as weak and helpless and make you their caregivers.

Jealous of your success
They are never happy when you win and want all your wins for themselves instead. These toxic friends will make you feel like you're not enough to even after

achieving a remarkable feat. They will compare you to others.

They belittle you
It may come off as a joke, but they will subtly tell you that there are certain things you can't achieve.

They are Untrustworthy
You cannot trust them with your properties or secrets.

They Try to Change You
They are always on the quest to change and make you more like themselves. Whether it be your hairstyle, clothes, or the people you date.

They don't like your other friends
Whenever you hang out with them, they make a big deal of it and accuse you of abandoning them for your other friends. They never agree to go with you to spend time with your other friends. They want you for themselves only. Their insecurity could cause this, but it'll get to a point where it is borderline toxic.

They demand all your attention: You can never have alone time or time to see your other friends. They want to be all up in your space 24/7 and have no respect for your privacy or boundaries.

Improving a toxic friendship isn't a walk in the park. You can either try to make it work or end it. If you bring your grievances to them and they make you feel like you're overreacting, that is a sign that they never cared about you in the first place. A true friend is willing to change and apologize if they ever did anything wrong to you.

When this doesn't happen, the best thing to do is end the friendship. You have nothing to lose and everything to gain.

Getting Out Of a Toxic Relationship & Getting Over a Toxic Relationship

Leaving a toxic relationship can be heartbreaking, but it is necessary to save yourself from a house that has been set ablaze.

The Steps to leaving a toxic relationship are as follows:

Take Responsibility
This is you accepting that you are not 100% perfect and that you may have also contributed to the toxicity brewing in the relationship. However, this may not always be the case because some people do not need to be triggered before they show their true colors.

Talk Things Out
They may not even be aware of the harm they cause you in the relationship, so having a conversation about this with them is recommended. Tell them how they make you feel, and watch out for them to respond. If they seem unconcerned, they never loved you in the first place. Hard pill to swallow, but it's the truth.

Also, if they show concern and promise to change, you have something to work with. You will know they are genuinely sorry because remorse cannot be hidden. If this is the case, you can draft out new ways to do things and ensure that those bad things are never repeated.

Look for counsel from a third party
If, after you have taken responsibility and tried to talk to them, they refuse to be corrected, then the next thing to do is get an opinion from a trusted source. It can be anyone that you hold in high esteem.

Call it Quits
This is the last step. Walk away and stay firm with your decision to do so. It will only take time for them to run back, begging for forgiveness. You can forgive them but never take them back when they do so. You can do better, and you deserve someone treating you like a queen. Do not settle for less. They will not be the last partner on earth for you.

Finally, be reminded that you have nothing to lose when you leave a toxic relationship. Instead, you have everything to gain. The most important of them is peace of mind.

Getting Over a Toxic Relationship

Leaving a toxic relationship does not guarantee that you will automatically move on from it. Getting over a person you once loved can be an extreme sport, and here's what you can do to soothe the situation.

Focus on Self-care and Self-love
Who better than you can love and care for yourself? Love yourself, care for yourself and always put yourself first. When you are irrevocably in love with yourself, you will see that you don't let anyone into your life.

Don't Jump into a New Relationship
A huge mistake is to use a new relationship to forget the last. You do not have a new partner but some alone time with yourself.

Get a Hobby
Getting a hobby is a great diversion. Choose something you like to do or have been wanting to try for a while. You must occupy your time and put your effort to use if you genuinely want to get over the toxic relationship. Those who participated in hobbies are less likely to experience stress and depressive symptoms. Choosing an athletic activity such as running, swimming, football, or even gymnastics can significantly help.

Lastly, if they love you, they will do whatever it takes to work things out.

How Staying In Toxic Relationships Affects Your Feminine Energy

Your feminine energy has to be protected at all costs. Feminine energy is divine and gracious, and toxicity is its enemy.

Staying in a toxic relationship as a woman who wants to claim her energy is the wrong step. Love and emotions in intimate relationships move feminine energy, and when this is lacking, the power cannot survive.

Your feminine energy is responsible for empathy and nature and guides you toward living from our hearts. It can be wounded in a toxic relationship, thus leaving you too attached with low self-worth, victimhood, and a need always to be saved. A woman with unwounded feminine energy in a healthy relationship will have a high sense of self-worth and confidence in her skin and craft.

We have come to the end of this chapter. You must have already known if you're in a toxic relationship or friendship. If you're not, that's great, but if you are, it's great too because now you know what to do.

"Mitchell, leave that man!"

CHAPTER ELEVEN

How To Utilize The Best of Your Feminine Energy

"Every time you improve your sensuality, you increase your feminine energy, beauty, and wisdom." - Lebo Grand.

Dating can be a lot to take in, especially in the first few weeks or months. Your emotions are over the roof, your sensory overloads are higher than usual, and anything your partner does has a high potential of taking you down the rabbit hole or, if you're lucky, up the skies into cloud nine.

Utilizing your feminine energy in the best way possible to get the most favorable outcome from your relationships is a must! If you want your relationship to be fruitful and to stand the test of them, you must incorporate your feminine energy into it, and your power shouldn't be left behind.

I noticed a dynamic change since I started incorporating feminine energy into my relationships. I was happier, and my partner was delighted as well, and when we eventually broke things off, it was mutual. We both understood that we wanted different things out of life, and thus we broke things off to go our separate ways.

Another thing worthy of noting is that only your feminine energy will not cut. If you are in a relationship with someone who has not yet begun working on their energies, then I'm afraid you have a long way to go. When your energy matches your partner's, there comes a synergy, a oneness that will help the two of you stand the test of time.

How to be in Your Feminine Energy With Your Partner

If you want to deepen or widen your horizon with your partner, you must learn to be in your feminine energy with them.

Ask Them For Help
I like to go to my partner for help, be it advice, money, or whatever. It makes them feel involved in your life. This does not mean bugging them for things you can do yourself, and the point is to let them help you once in a while.

Flirting Should Not Stop After The Relationship Starts
Many women get this wrong. Keeping the spark alive by flirting or even seducing your partner is vital. It's fun to show that you're still attracted to them. Just dating them does not mean you no longer have to be sexy.

My boyfriend liked that I was feminine and not scared to express my feelings. I'd send him seductive photos and texts while he's at work to drive him over the edge. He loved it and would beg me never to stop.

Now, my boyfriend may not be like your partners, but the fact remains that people will get bored if their attention is not constantly being pricked at.

Be Unconstrained
Feminine energy is about taking risks and going outside the box. You don't have to be restricted or limited in your relationship with your partner. Don't let the fun or the fire in your relationship die out. When your partner sees that you are trying to keep the fire burning, it encourages them to do the same. Be open to new experiences. Be curious to explore the world.

Break Your Cycles
This means looking closely at your previous relationships. Study the cycles and patterns. It'll help you not to make the same mistake again. When you study the ways, you'll be able to decipher when it begins to happen again.

While you study past partners and the relationships you had with them, you also have to put yourself up for examination. We are not all perfect, and as much as we try to convince ourselves that we are not the problem, we sometimes end up being precisely the problem. If you ever discover that you are the problem, take measures to change and conquer those patterns. If you don't, you'll go into a new relationship, and the cycle will repeat itself.

If you're unsure how to break this cycle, then embracing your feminine energy is the right help you need. When you utilize this energy, it will help bring out the best in your relationships.

How to be in Your Feminine Energy With Your Family

It is not a secret that many of us come from broken homes, and I am not left out. My family was pretty good for a while, but it didn't stay that way for long. Most of you did not even have a happy childhood, and those who did, are out there questioning why everything has changed in this present time. We're adults, and we barely talk to our family members anymore.

Our feminine energy ensures that all broken relationships are mended and that our peace is restored.

Speak Their Language
You're embracing, and you don't know where to begin in terms of reconnecting with your family. Then one of the actions you have to take is to discover their language and speak it. All humans can be associated with the seven love languages: words of affirmation, acts of service, receiving gifts, physical touch, and quality time.

Love languages do not just pertain to romantic relationships, and suppose everyone on earth has to love language irrespective of their romantic status. In that case, they do not have to be romantically involved with you before you can begin loving them based on their language.

Words of Affirmation
When words of affirmation are a person's love language, they thrive in spoken affection and are happier when they are praised, complimented, and encouraged. Criticism and spiteful words can disrupt their flow for long periods.

Look around your family and decide who thrives more on words of affirmation. Then, please give it to them. Compliment them, encourage them, and then see how drawn they'll be to you.

Acts of Service
This language best describes doing something for someone you know would love, especially without being asked to. People with this love language will be overly joyful at your thoughtful gestures. If your father's love language is acts of service, do expect him to grin from ear to ear when you wash his car out of the blue.

Receiving Gifts
Gifting your loved ones generic gifts may not cut. This love language has to do with thoughtful gifts. For example, gifting them a snack after a rough day may bring out the waterworks, but giving them a dress when they already have tons of it may not get them so excited. Usually, the thought is put into the gift that counts. So, try it out today. Let your feminine energy lead you.

Physical Touch
Since we are dealing with family here, we must be careful about this. There is an obvious line that family members around themselves cannot cross, but a simple warm hug can be all it takes to make a gray day turn into a bright one.

Quality Time
This language is associated with attention, presence, and togetherness. It has to do with expressing your love by actively listening to them. Your mother loves talking, but there's no one there to listen to her? Be the one who listens and gives her the attention she needs. Put down your phone and listen while they talk.

Loving a person the right way can break their defenses no matter how hard they seem. Consistency is key to the best results.

When you do the activities mentioned above with your family, you can expect a 100 percent change in your relationship with your family. Speak in everyone's love language as often as possible, then watch how the dynamics change.

Remember that you must be on the same page for your feminine energy to blossom. Your energy will not flourish as long as you still have pent-up anger and hurt from the past.

How to be in Your Feminine Energy at Work

It's time to stop competing with men and embrace your unique feminine skills and intelligence.

Between the 1930s and mid-1970s, women began to work in the labor force, and their numbers kept growing, with a high percent of single women and a low percentage of married women in 1970. As time went on, they began demanding to be treated equally with men, and for their business to succeed, they believed they had to be like men. Sadly, this meant they had to leave much of their femininity behind and adapt to only their masculine energy.

"Trying to be a man is a waste of a woman," Sarah Jessica Parker.

Here are some tips for being in your feminine energy at work.

Recognize Your Strengths And Weakness
When you recognize your strengths, it'll be easier for you to develop them and stop trying so hard to compete with others at your place of work. Understanding and acknowledging your weaknesses as well is essential. You'll stop fighting pointless battles with your male colleagues when you know these things.

Listen to Your Intuition
I worked in a counterpart company for six months after college because I thought it was what I wanted. I loved the 9-5 lifestyle and was eager to join in. It was difficult because everyone in the office hated their job, and it told me. It was months later that I realized I could not be a little ray of sunshine for people obsessed with the rain. I started listening to myself and eventually changed my job. Lastly, listening to your intuition when your logical sense of reasoning is saying otherwise can be difficult, but it is doable. You won't always get it right, but sometimes, you may.

Dress the Part
Stop trying hard to look like a man. If it's your style and you're comfortable with it then, that's completely fine but, going out of your way to look like your male colleagues is a no-no if you're trying to bring out more of your feminine energy. Corporate companies may have strict dress codes, but you can always tweak them a little.

Be feminine. Wear a brightly-colored dress, and rock it with heels. Get a feminine scent you like and stick with it. It's time to embrace your feminine side wholly.

Show Empathy
The female energy is emotional, so you can bring empathy to work. The idea that there is no room for

emotions is wrong and should be abolished. People want to feel heard and understood, so empathy is instrumental in pursuing success.

Be Cooperative
This means establishing a form of togetherness in the workplace and working together in peace and harmony—a form of cooperation void of envy, jealousy, and competition. The masculine energy tends to lean on the "I did" part of things; meanwhile, the feminine energy leans towards the "We did" part.

Support Other Women
Equality at work cannot be gained if we keep downgrading our genders. We must show support and that women can be women's best friends. If we want to be taken seriously, we have to act the part.

Impacts of Ignoring Your Feminine Energy at Work

There are numerous consequences of ignoring your feminine energy at work, so let's look at them.

- It reduces your potential.

- **We begin to over-give**
This means agreeing to everything that is required of us, even if it means ourselves, because we are trying to prove that we belong there, and as a result, we can do whatever is required of us just like our male counterparts.

- **We lose connection with our bodies:** Us women tend to forget how our hormones work. There are a lot of factors that affect us as women (menstruation, menopause, e.t.c). The masculine energy does not understand the dynamics of our hormonal behaviorism, which is why we must embrace feminine energy.

• When you ignore your feminine energy at work, you will become unhappy and overwhelmed by the changes your body undergoes. In addition, you will lack fulfillment while struggling for acceptance.

Some Signs That Your Masculine Energy has Overridden Your Feminine Energy at work.

• You always feel bad or guilty when you try to take a break, even after working for a long time.

• You are always in competition mode.

• You judge and talk down on yourself for being too sensitive and emotional.

• There is a massive gap between intuition and logical reasoning; sometimes, your instinct may be non-existent altogether.

In conclusion, women should endeavor to take our feminine energy to work with us daily. It would be best if you didn't leave it at home.

How to be in Your Feminine Energy Around Your Male Friends

In high school, I used to always roll with boys. They were my friends, and I liked their companionship compared to females. Due to this, I started acting like one of them. I wasn't that girl anymore who needed a new circle because she had been stabbed in the back too many times by her female friends. I was a dude now because I was always surrounded by masculine energy. My male friends then used to refer to me as one of them.

"She's one of us," they'll say. "She's our man."

As time passed, I gradually lost my feminine energy as a girl. I don't think it is mentioned enough how hanging out with boys often can cause us to lose our feminine energy. We all have feminine and masculine energy, and because I was just a teen who didn't know any better, I was leaning too deep into my masculine energy because of the friends I was hanging out with. This is why it is essential for there to be a sort of balance between both energies.

A month later, I decided enough was enough as I stopped hanging out a lot with them, and I watched myself get back in form with my feminine energy.

Embracing your feminine energy is the key to a lasting relationship with your partners, family, co-workers, and friends. It would help if you didn't overlook this.

Let's see how you can be in your feminine energy around your male friends proper:

- Be true to yourself: Try as much as possible to give your opinions from a feminine point of view.
- Avoid competitions.
- Be soft.

CHAPTER TWELVE

UNLEARNING THE MYTHS ABOUT FEMININITY

"A myth is a religion in which no one any longer believes." –James Feibleman.

Over the years, many people have been vocal about what they think feminine energy is all about. While some are true and indeed facts, others are entirely false. And for you to effectively step into your feminine energy as a black, bold, and beautiful woman, you must do it right and learn from the right source.

Some myths are:

Feminine energy is female energy.
This is not true. As said before, feminine energy is NOT only present in women. Everyone has both energies embedded in them and needs both to navigate through life. The feminine energy is empathic, experiencing, compassionate, affectionate, warm, welcoming, attractive, receptive, graceful, sensual, and relaxing. Society has had a way of attributing these characteristics to women only. Still, some men tend to show some of these qualities too, which indicates that they also drop into their feminine energy from time to time.

In the same way, some women are more in touch with their masculine energy, which is doing, achieving, organizing, thinking, analyzing, competing, and making logical points. Men who drop into their feminine tend to be caring, loving, and welcoming, but that does not mean they cannot be stern when needed. So, feminine energy is not for women alone. Men can also connect with this energy, and it doesn't make them less male.

Feminine energy is soft
We need to understand that softness is part of feminine energy, and yes, sometimes, when a need arises for us to be soft, we will. But that is not all there is. Feminine energy combines different things, and softness is part of it. The feminine is also powerful, but only when it is necessary to be. A perfect example is Mother Nature; we see her softness in creation–the seas, the soft wind, the cool breeze, oceans, flowers, trees, et al. But we also see how powerful/destructive she can get–tornadoes, hurricanes, floods, etc.

However, some women have been taught from their early years to be masculine because it is complicated and challenging, making them harden themselves and refuse to drop into their femininity. One thing you need to understand is feminine energy is all about you. It's inside of you, and how you choose to navigate all of what makes its entirety depends on you. So, sis, you can choose to be soft or challenging, depending on the need to be one or the other, as long as you're not hiding under a masculine silhouette.

Feminine energy is girly
This is another myth we need to rule out of our lives.

Feminine energy is a state of being. All the characteristics which make it up do not need to be in skirts to be activated. For some of us, dresses, red lipsticks, and bright colors are external vessels that we use to express this state of being. And it works for us. But does the fact that it works for some people and doesn't work for some mean they cannot access their feminine energies? The answer is no. It's not about the colors or choice of clothes; it's about you and how you choose to express it. When we look at it more realistically, these things do not have meaning until you give them to them. A lady who loves nude lipsticks and straight brown gowns can connect her feminine energy core well. Another lady who wears pink daily can operate from the deep center of her masculine energy. So, these things don't matter if pink dresses and red lipsticks make you feel more feminine! If it doesn't, no stress. The main concern is whether you have dropped into your feminine energy and how effectively you use your powers.

Feminine energy is only used to attract male attention
This myth is why many of us have refused to drop into our feminine energy. But this is only a myth—it's not true! Feminine energy attracts different kinds of people your way. It is attractive energy, but it DOES NOT attract male attention only. It opens you up to beautiful friendships and connections from both genders because you will always be in touch with your emotional and soft sides and others.

And trust me, there is nothing more beautiful than a woman wanting something and attracting it to herself. There's nothing more glorious than a woman bringing life and warmth to everyone she makes contact with.

There's nothing more wonderful than a woman lighting up the room with her presence and feminine eminence. So, yes, you would attract attention and have to get used to it. But that is not the only reason we preach about feminine energy. Flush this myth down the drain.

Feminine energy only receives
Most women who have been in their masculine energies for a long time tend to believe this fallacy that to drop into your feminine energy means to always be at the receiving end. Note the word, always.

This is a myth that needs to be dropped. Feminine energy is attractive, and people will always want to draw close to you and offer you gifts. But note that feminine energy is also empathic energy. This means that you will provide when a situation requires you to give. The feminine opens to love, and love is both giving and receiving. Your partner buying you a bracelet is an expression of love, the same way you getting him a cologne or his favorite brand of shoes is.

Giving and receiving can be fluid too—only when you're in your feminine do you give out of empathy or when there is a need to, and not necessarily from a place of control or because it makes you feel superior.

Feminine energy is docile
What does being docile mean? To be easily led or controlled. And because feminine energy is fluid, people think you can easily toss and turn people who embody this energy. But this is not true. I'd rather say feminine energy is passive when it needs to be. This means you have the ability/chance to do something but decide not to because it does not help the situation. Empathy, remember? Let me give an example. Say your partner gets home from work tired and hungry. You notice a drop in his countenance and offer to tell him stories or sing to him, and he declines and tells you to leave him alone. Now, you would leave him, not because he asked you to, per se, but because, at that moment, that was what needed to be done.

Now, you were not controlled by him. You were only paying attention to details and making the right decision for both of you. You could have decided to throw tantrums and yell, but you were calmer. Feminine energy comes with emotional mastery.

When we tap into it, we realize that we flow because we have a better understanding of and connection with our emotions, making us handle situations better.

Women need to always be in their feminine energy
This is so not true. You do not need to throw the other under the bus for one to thrive. Adequate amounts of both points must be in a person to achieve balance.

It would help if you dropped into your feminine when you need to get creative, feel, learn, explore your sides and be.

It would help if you dropped into your masculine when you needed to get things done, complete tasks, hit targets, and do.

Suppose you're too much in your feminine. In that case, you'd always relax and allow people to do things for you; you pay attention to people to the extent that they feel super safe around you, you connect deeply with the feelings of others, you're vulnerable and transparent to a fault —all of which are great until They are not. The downsides are picking and keeping more energy than you need to, and you might eventually lose yourself. You may never really get anything done because you have a significant amount of help. You may even get lazy and never accomplish anything.

If you're too much in your masculine, you'd always have eyes on the prize, never lose focus, constantly strategize, hustle without feeling burnt out, and your drive is second to none. The downsides are everything might become a competition to you, you sulk when you don't achieve one thing even though you have tons of achievements, you are quickly disappointed at yourself or other people, you give too much, and you may lose out on relevant information because people will think, "oh well, she has it all figured out, so she may not need it."

This is the reason you need to balance both parts of you. As women, we do not ALWAYS need to be in our feminine energies. Imagine relaxing when you ought to be preparing for a presentation at work. You will fail woefully, and feminine energy won't take the blame—you will. Because you could not decipher which energy was needed for what and when to apply which.

Masculine energy is more powerful than feminine

The patriarchal society has successfully painted feminine energy as weaker and "not enough." So many women have been taught to believe that true power comes with activating your masculinity. But there is no basis to compare the both because both make a perfect complementary team. In her video on Understanding Feminine Energy, Alexandra Villarroel Abrego describes both in a more relatable manner. She said that you use both energies from the moment you wake up till you lay your head.

When you wake up in the morning, your mind starts to work: you have a picture or visualization of how your day would be, the places you'll go, the things you'd do—that's the feminine.

The moment you get up and start doing all of the things you visualized, the moment you start taking action, that's the masculine.

Now here's the drill.

If you take action without picturing it carefully in your head, there's a problem.

If you imagine or create things in your mind without taking action, there's also a problem.

So you see, there's no question of which is more powerful. We need both to live in a world like ours.

Dropping into your feminine energy stops you from being a feminist

I came across this recently, and I went, "Oh my God!" because it took me off-balance immediately after I read it. This is such a ridiculous lie, and I'd tell you why. First, what is feminism? Feminism is the belief that men and women should have equal rights and opportunities socially, economically, and politically.

Feminine energy does not, in any way, preach against any principle that feminism upholds. How does taking time to relax and rest make you less of a feminist? How does being in touch with your emotions stop you from exercising equal rights as your male counterparts? And the reason this myth still goes on because people still believe feminine energy is soft and anybody that steps into it can be controlled. But you know better now. It does not even get in the way at all. And trust me when I say this is another patriarchal imprint that some women have carried with them all their lives and has made them refuse to drop into their feminine. Most are still plagued with the assertion that they must be like men to do things. This imbalance and false knowledge have left us with successful yet burnt-out women. You can be in touch with both energies and still be a feminist. Yes, you can!

How can you unlearn these myths?

Unlearning these myths is a critical aspect of stepping into your femininity. Maybe you have held onto some of these myths for a long time and don't think you can let go of them. Perhaps some of these myths were imposed on you, and you find it hard to detach yourself from them.

Maybe you have other reasons for holding on to them. But I want you to understand that they are LIES. And no matter how long you keep believing a lie, it will never be true. So, you have to unlearn. According to the Cambridge dictionary, to unlearn is to try to forget your usual way of doing something to learn a new and sometimes better way.

Here are some things you can do to unlearn these myths:

Be open to new knowledge
You have to be ready to ditch the old knowledge that you've carried and learn new ones as long as they make you better. It would help if you were willing to unlearn and learn. You can not place new content in an already-filled cup; it must first be empty. The same thing applies here too. Open yourself up to learn what feminine energy

is genuinely about, not what your mother, uncle, or brother told you. A famous phrase says when there is a will, there is a way. If you are willing to unlearn, then trust me, you will.

Be more curious
The best learners ask questions. When we were younger, we usually questioned everything around us.

We wanted to know why the sky was blue and the earth was brown. Everything was new to us, and so we craved clarity. Some of us retained all that knowledge, called them principles, and allowed them to guide us into adulthood. These pieces of information, when compiled, make the real us. But the world changes with each clock tick, and we can't stay behind. Maybe these "myths" (as we call them now) were helpful before, but we cannot continue to grow old and worn-out boats on new waters– we will sink. Ask questions and keep renewing your mind You cannot afford to be left behind.

Change your location
Sometimes, we may need to change our current environment to unlearn these myths. Unlearning is a psychological process, and whether we agree or not, our environment plays a vital role in shaping our lives. Move from the familiar places and people (who may want to hold on to these myths and limit your victory over them.

Surround yourself with women with high feminine energy
If you've thought these myths are true, then there is a high chance that you have been around men(and women) who embody masculine energy more. If you pay close attention, you will notice that most myths paint feminine

energy as weak. And because females tend to tilt more in the feminine direction, you need to surround yourself with more women who are in touch with their feminine energies. Listening to their words and watching their actions would go a long way to speed up your unlearning process and help you achieve balance.

Reflect
Look within yourself. Understand who your person is; your wants, desires, fears, and abilities. One reason people allow just any information and believe just anything is that they don't know who they are. They are torn between nature and nurture and find it hard to differentiate between characteristics that belong to them and characteristics that they were made to pick.

Ask yourself questions like: Do I naturally tilt to the masculine or feminine parts of my life(nature), or was I taught to wear specific energy(nurture) even though that was not who I was?

Answering these questions would help you unlearn certain myths because now, you have a clearer understanding of yourself, you know why you behave the way you do, what you can accommodate, and most importantly, you know your truth.

As said before, feminine energy is all about you and how you can harness or express it depending on situations as you go through life.

Set boundaries
Unlearning is not as arduous as it seems, and it all depends on your willingness and determination. And this is why you need to filter the information your mind

receives and keeps. You do not need everything you hear. While draining these lies from your mind, you need to be cautious of what fills your mind again, so you don't keep repeating the process.

Go for therapy
Although this may sound too extreme, many women have been so immersed in these falsehoods that they may need help for their unlearning process to be complete and adequate. Maybe you have tried to follow the procedures listed above, and it does not seem to work, or you have not even tried because you don't see yourself having any beliefs other than the ones you already have. If this is you, it's beautiful. Don't be scared or try to beat yourself up. That you even made an effort to correct the wrong screams progress! You need an extra push–a professional one and you will be back on track before you know it.

CHAPTER THIRTEEN

FEIGNING STRENGTH IN WEAKNESS

"Life isn't about being strong or pretending we are strong to impress others. It takes courage to be authentic with our feelings and acknowledge that real strength comes from recognizing our moments of weakness. - Yong Kang Chan"

You do not need to fake strength in weakness. Sometimes pretending to be tough is a sign of weakness, and being someone you're not is not a quality of feminine energy. Yes, it is beneficial to have strength during trials and challenges, but not to the point where it turns into blatant pretense.

It's fragile to refuse assistance when you need it. Stop behaving like you are an expert and seek help.

I remember being out with one of my male friends one night. We were out to get some groceries. (Yeah, grocery shopping at night seems odd, but we were leading irregular lives then.) Anyway, when we were done, we got out and were putting our stuff in the car boot when my friend noticed a middle-aged woman trying desperately to get her car door open while, at the same time, holding a bunch of things in both hands. My friend walked over to her and offered to help, and she refused. He was visibly dazzled by her refusal because she looked like she needed help. So, he provides again, and she refuses, this time in an angry tone. My friend shrugged and walked back to the car. I watched the whole thing unfold from the car.

As we were revering from the parking lot into the street, we heard a rain of cuss from her direction, she had tripped, and all the stuff she was holding went down along with her. It was a hilarious sight and one that could have been avoided if only she had allowed someone to help.

It's the same way with a lot of us. We refuse help because of our egos and a misconception of feminine energy.

It takes strength and courage to acknowledge that you need help. So, you should be proud if you have that ability.

There is something called an Apprentice Mindset.

Since the beginning, an apprenticeship mindset has been the key to extraordinary success. Now, while this book isn't about making wealth and being successful, it causes no harm if we dive into that for a few bit. Being a prosperous, muscular black woman doesn't get any better.

As the name implies, the apprenticeship mindset is an established set of attitudes established by a person to gain new knowledge, skills, and behaviors to improve their competency in their chosen field.

The Apprenticeship Mindset ensures that you Never Stop Acquiring New Knowledge.

One of the ways to increase your feminine energy is to unleash your creativity. How can you do that? Acquiring knowledge and actively engaging in self-growth is the key to fulfilling and genuinely being in your feminine energy.

To live our lives to the fullest, we must constantly seek ways to improve them. It is not enough to stay in your comfort zone. You must leave that zone, come out, and look for ways to improve yourself.

Some benefits of acquiring new knowledge

You will be more fulfilled.
I think the feeling of fulfillment is not emphasized enough for people's understanding. It is a feeling of happiness and satisfaction and a happy, contented feeling. Getting to experience such a feeling should not be underrated, and the measure one has to go through to get it should not be looked down on.

Do not settle with just about any life because you are tired of fighting for a better tomorrow for yourself. You deserve more. A lot more. Sitting in one place and managing a mediocre life should be criminal. There's so much opportunity for you if you decide to step out of your comfort zone and take charge of your life. To attain fulfillment in this aspect, you must try as much as possible never to stop acquiring new knowledge.

It Helps You to Gain New Perspective
One great way to start appreciating and comprehending the world on a different level is to read more books or learn new skills.

One must be open-minded in a culture with as much diversity as ours. Learning a new language, for example, can influence how you perceive the world. Once you know something new, the world seldom ever changes.

You will also find it simpler to engage with others due to your improved understanding and appreciation of other people's viewpoints and opinions. You'll be closer to developing the apprenticeship mindset because you're constantly eager to learn new things.

It Will Humble You
Trying to act like you are an expert on everything will hurt you. You will go through life uninformed and arrogant, and you will get more modest as you uncover new knowledge you weren't familiar with. Learning can humble you, and if you keep an open mind, every interaction is a chance to learn something new.

Enhances the quality of your life
Learning new things can improve your quality of life in various ways. Some people know something and then misapply it. On the other side, you can utilize the excellent knowledge you have acquired daily and perhaps even share your expertise with others to benefit society.

Making informed judgments and developing a better understanding and awareness of your surroundings and society are made possible by gaining new knowledge, which ultimately improves the quality of your life.

The Apprenticeship Mindset Improves Your Listening/Asking Question Skills

A long time ago, I was at a summit for climate change. The hall was packed with men and women from God knows where. Undoubtedly, everyone knows at least one thing about climate change. Still, at that summit, everyone was excited to put away everything they thought they knew about the subject of the program and focus on the knowledge they would acquire.

Listening plays a huge role in not feigning strength when you are weak. Helpful information can come from any source, and when you try to act like you know it all (affecting force), you lose a chance at learning.

You cannot cultivate an apprenticeship mindset when you are not open to listening.

Asking questions is also a crucial key worthy of note if you want to establish an apprenticeship mindset. A curious person will never be found lacking knowledge. They are always asking questions, burning with the desire to know. I understand that not everyone is born with a curious mind, but it can be cultivated. Women, especially the ones that are trying to step into their energies to have a curious mind,

We learn a lot more if we ask good questions, which means there are bad and good questions. It would help if you wasted no time asking frivolous questions, and questions that will not positively affect your life should be avoided at all costs.

Asking questions leads to building emotional intelligence. Take, for example, a company that provides services for the masses and asks questions of its customers about the quality of its services. The feedback they get will make them more emotionally intelligent and aware of what they lack and which services need to be worked on.

Emotional intelligence is the ability to see things from other people's perspectives. When you ask questions (be it about any subject), you can get answers from different points of view.

Benefits Of Listening and Asking Questions

You can successfully develop connections based on trust and sustainability by paying attention to others. It fosters a sense of connection and respect in intimate and professional interactions.

Listening is the doorway to understanding. It is something that the world is missing today, and a lot of lives have been lost because of simple misunderstandings.

Listening also promotes intimacy and is an excellent way of improving intimacy levels. So, sisters, it's time to begin listening rather than always speaking.

Asking questions has its benefits. From acquiring more knowledge to eliminating confusion, the list is endless.

Years ago, I mentally dissed a particular person because I had misheard them. Everyone must have experienced this before.

I had heard them say something about me while drinking with a few friends. Even though it was noisy, I was sure they had condescendingly spoken to me. I was furious, but I maintained composure until we left the location. As soon as I arrived at my house, I blocked and deleted their phone number, and in addition, I unfollowed and blocked them on social media.

Although it was a stupid move, I was a strong-willed woman who wouldn't stand for being disrespected. A few weeks later, I ran into them and was furious with myself for doing so. They told me they had been attempting to contact me all along and would have assumed that I had blocked them if they had known any better.

I was embarrassed and felt foolish. While dissing them, they were utterly oblivious to what was happening.

I told them I had a problem with my service provider before leaving. I unblocked their phone numbers and social media accounts when I got home before sending them a message. They were so happy and grateful that I could finally get to them. At this moment, I could not hold it in any longer, so I expressed my displeasure with what they had stated that evening at the hangout. They were surprised and then told me the precise words they had said. To my surprise, it turned out that they were complimenting me for something I had done.

I felt foolish and embarrassed far more strongly than I did earlier that day. I had no choice but to retract my rash charge. The fact that I could have gotten angry at them for what I thought I heard said more about me than about them.

If I had merely asked a simple question, all of that stress I put myself through might have been avoided.

Situations, where a simple question could have prevented a lot of mayhem are endless. It is, therefore, essential to ask questions. Feigning knowledge in times of ignorance is wrong!

The Apprenticeship mindset helps you cultivate healthy behaviors (Mindsets and Attitudes)

Cultivating a Healthy Mindset

Accepting yourself for who you are: The concept of self-love cannot be overemphasized. This concept has already been explained broadly in this book. So, you must already have an idea of what it entails. Feigning strength in weakness is not a sign of a person who has accepted themselves as they are. The Apprenticeship Mindset is an attitude you have to establish by yourself, and one of them is taking you for who you are.

Appreciating the little things: We live in a fast world that's not stopping for anything or anyone. Before it moves past you, I want you to take your time to appreciate the little things around you. It could just be enjoying that it's a sunny day or a little flower growing between the cracks of a wall.

Other little things can also be something that nurtures and sustains you. Anything that gives you the slightest glimpse of happiness is worth appreciating.

Someone optimistic, kind, lively, and cheerful is an example of a person who appreciates the little things in life.

Talk about your feelings: Talking about your feelings validates what you are experiencing. Too many of us tend to ignore our feelings and suffer in silence. This is not a way to cultivate a healthy mindset. You must understand that feelings will disappear if you do not address them. They'll always be there, pilling up, and one day, when these feelings are triggered, they'll come rushing out.

It's better to talk about them the moment they surface. Begin tackling them each time they come up.

Talking about your feelings will lower the effect of those feelings. I remember when I got heartbroken. The feeling was so intense that I had difficulty breathing. I cried all night, but it didn't soothe the pain. Let me add that crying solves nothing, and you can't shout your pain or sorrows away. If anything, it makes the pain hurt worse.

I went to my best friend's early the following morning to talk. I knew at that time the importance of venting. Upon meeting her, I narrated my ordeal, and she encouraged me to stay strong. She assured me I would be okay, and I believed her. In no time, I was up on my feet again.

Although the hurt was still there, it wasn't as intense as the previous night.

Don't suffer alone. Open up to someone about how you feel.

Lead a Healthier Lifestyle
There are numerous activities to take on that will help you lead a healthy lifestyle. Picking the ones you know will benefit you is the first step.

It is unreasonable to quit alcohol when you don't have a drinking problem in the first place. The bottom line is picking a healthy lifestyle that is particular to you.

Some general healthy lifestyles include:

- Getting plenty of rest
- Eating a balanced diet
- Drinking more water
- Avoiding energy vampire
- Practicing self-care
- Incorporating more food and vegetables into your diet.
- Exercising

All these are necessary for cultivating a good and healthy mindset.

Reduce Screen Time: This is a problem I also struggle with. It is almost impossible to avoid it. There's a screen on the train, the street, the airport, restaurants, etc. Our eyes and ears are constantly engaged. We receive information that we did not ask for daily, and in the process, our mindset is altered and made to change into what the world wants it to be. So, how do we combat this menace?

A great piece of advice would be to move away from civilization and live under a rock! But we can't do that now, can we? We cannot thoroughly fight this, and we can only try our best to control what we allow into our minds.

Taking a few minutes to meditate and detox your mind can do wonders. Listening to soothing music in your alone time can also work. Set a time limit on social media so it reminds you to log off. This can be pretty challenging. I know this because I tried it before, but consistency ultimately wins.

Positively Impact the lives of those around you: Do you want to cultivate a healthy mindset? Then you also have to extend a hand to those around you. Led them to the light that you have found. Stand up for a cause that you believe in. Do you have a soft spot for the Girl Power movement? Join the trend, then. Let your passion drive you. Be impactful. Be kind.

Smiling more often at people also has a positive impact. Also, smiling can't be so hard. Ask questions, remember the names of people you've met, listen to them talk, offer a helping hand, and show kindness to those around you.

In conclusion, cultivating a Healthy Mindset will involve your physical, emotional, mental, and sometimes, spiritual input.

Cultivating a Healthy Attitude
Attitude is a settled way of thinking or feeling about something, and it is often the result of our experience and upbringing.

There are negative and positive attitudes. My focus here is to show you how to develop a positive attitude toward situations around you.

Change your Perception: Since attitude can often result from our experience and upbringing, it only makes sense that this should be the first step.

You may have had a bad experience with something that completely changed how you see that thing, changing your perception by trying to pick something positive from that experience.

Volunteer
Volunteering encourages selflessness. It is healthy for the soul to assist others. Studies have shown that being charitable extends our love and makes us happy. When faced with challenges, you can become downcast and withdraw into your shell, but expanding your perspective can assist you in adopting a healthy attitude while promoting happiness throughout your society.

Volunteering is one of the most challenging yet rewarding adventures to take on in your life.

Examine the Healthy Attitudes of People you Admire
Who is your mentor? Who are the people who motivate you? Examine their healthy attitude and emulate it if you feel it is worthy of being copied.

Avoid Unhealthy Relationships
Nothing will disrupt your healthy attitude faster than an unhealthy relationship. Most women like to stick with terrible partners because they think they can change them. When changing them, they end up burnt out and unconsciously develop a bad attitude towards things they experienced in the relationship.

It's one thing to be supportive and another to be a grown adult's savior. While you're busy looking after them, who looks after you?

A healthy attitude is not something you can immediately cultivate. Developing a healthy attitude involves making small changes in your daily routine.

Creating a healthy mindset is not something you should do all at once. Start small, and you'll amass much of it as time progresses. Instead of spending your morning on the internet, how about doing something productive to help you achieve your daily goals?

Instead of binging on unhealthy snacks, you can eat better meals.

Do you see how it goes? These little things are the things that will change your life.

CHAPTER FOURTEEN

Be The Woman Who Takes Charge

"If you must excel, you have to master the act of taking charge of the things that concern you."

Being in charge, in this context, means accepting the responsibility to be responsible for yourself.

There are different areas to take charge of as a woman who is embracing her feminine energy, and they include;

- Taking charge of your finances
- Taking charge of your relationships
- Taking charge of your well-being/health
- Taking charge of your future/life
- Taking charge of your happiness
- Taking Charge Of Your Finances

It is no secret that men dominate the financial sector in the modern world. Men dominate everything from financial planning to investments. Although it can be challenging, some women have shown that it is possible to change the system. The lists are endless.

From Tiffany Alice to Olayinka Fadirepo, they are paving the way for other women to rule this industry and change how we view money.

Here are a few points to note if you're a woman looking to take control of your finances.

Learn about Finances

Although you may have already received instruction in a college or high school, studying on your own will produce positive results and make you more knowledgeable. There is something called financial literacy. As a woman who wants to take charge, you must work hard to get what you want.

The most fantastic method to build confidence to handle your money wisely and have a deposit that will keep you out of difficulty is learning about personal finances and gaining more knowledge on the subject. There are numerous courses online that you can take if you are interested in taking things a notch higher.

Have SMART Financial Goals for your future: SMART is an acronym for Specific, Measurable, Attainable, Relevant, and Time-bound.

Specific Goal

This entails knowing what you want to achieve. For what purpose do you save? It goes more than just piling money into your account. What are your plans for the money?

Measurable Goal

This has to do with numbers. How much do you want to save to achieve your specific goal? This way, you can know how much you have gotten and what's left to get.

Attainable

Is this goal achievable? Is it doable? Are you setting your expectations too high?

Relevant

Are your goals essential or proper? Are they relevant to you? Is it necessary?

Time-Bound
This means giving yourself a timeline to achieve this goal.

These are the SMART financial goals. If you want to take charge, you must follow these goals accordingly.

Debt Management
This is a way to get your debts under control through financial planning and budgeting. The essence of this is to help lower your current debts and also possibly help you eliminate incoming ones. Having a little debt here is not so bad, but it gets ugly when it begins to swallow you up.

If you are in too much debt, you must take debt management seriously. With proper planning and execution of those plans, you will begin to see the bright light at the end of the tunnel.

Regularly Check Your Credit Score
This is your most critical personal finance number.

Even if you're not applying for credit, it is still necessary to get used to constantly checking your credit score.

Build an Emergency Fund
You may think, 'I don't even have enough money to pay for my current expenses much more for a crisis.'

You are not required to make a sizable investment to start. You can begin modestly, and you must begin. This subheading says 'build,' but how do you build?

You progressively increase. Even though it can take years, the important thing is that you start; you never know when an emergency might happen.

Take Charge in your Relationship

Only you can create the kind of relationship you want, and you are the only one capable of making such a decision.

The most effective way to take charge of your relationship is first to take account of yourself. You cannot give what you don't have; therefore, you do not take charge when you haven't taken the lead or control of yourself.

It is your job to ensure your relationship turns out to be what you want it to be. If this isn't the case, it's in your hands to properly communicate these concerns with your partner.

Here are Ways You Can Take Charge of Your Relationship

Speak Up
Your voice is your power. Therefore, you have to use it. Giving the silent treatment or sulking around will not help matters. As a woman in her feminine energy, you have to be able to communicate your feelings in clear terms without being misunderstood. Tell your partner what you want or require from them in your romantic relationship.

Be Self-Sufficient
This means not being dependent on your partner and not allowing your world to revolve around them. You should be able to function in your world without them. Love can be strange sometimes, but you shouldn't lose your willpower and identity while falling in love. This is one of the ways to take charge.

Establish Boundaries
If there are no boundaries in a relationship, then anything is acceptable, which is wrong. You are two different individuals with different backgrounds, sometimes different cultures, religions, ethnicity, e.t.c, and you are brought together by love. But, as strong as love can be, boundaries must be set and put in place for that love to grow.

At the initial stage of the relationship, you may not quickly catch up with boundaries that need to be established because the love is still very active, but as time goes on, it'll begin to show.

Boundaries are healthy for your relationship. Be honest with what you need, listen to what your partner needs, and communicate respectfully.

Do Not Settle For Less
Many women end up with the wrong men because they permanently settle for less and are not ready to take charge as a woman. A woman who knows who she is will not settle for less. She always ends up with the person who is most deserving of her. Do not be afraid to make a choice. Do not condition yourself to think you are not worthy of a choice. Taking charge goes beyond just the physical, and it also has to do with your mental and emotional strength. Things will not always fall into your laps, but they will work fine if you stand your ground and take charge!

Take Charge of Your Well-being/Health
Taking charge of your well-being/wealth can be difficult if you are dealing with addiction, but if you've bought this book, it means you're on a journey to recovery.

You can gain control of your health by choosing a healthy lifestyle. Maintaining a diet and regularly exercising are some things you can do. A holistic approach to well-being can help you discover a lot of things and, perhaps, in the long run, your purpose.

You need to be responsible for your health, even if you have a chronic mental illness. It's self-management, taking charge of your condition and not letting it define you.

Here are some ways to take charge of your health and well-being

Get Adequate Sleep
You may have a crazy sleep schedule, but there's still time to cultivate a healthy one. Experts say adults should get at least 7 hours of sleep for a healthy life.

Cook your Food
This is important. Cooking your food yourself gives you a sense of responsibility. What better way to take charge than to cook your meals? If you don't cook, it's time to learn. It is never too late to learn. There are a lot of resources to teach you. (Cookbook and videos online). A woman stepping into her energy should be able to cook her meals. If she doesn't know how to do that, she should learn.

This is important because you will decide when selecting what to eat.

Go for a Regular Check-Up
Schedule an appointment with a physical examination doctor. Regular check-ups can help you detect diseases in their stages. You may not like seeing a doctor for anxiety

or other reasons, but you have to consider the benefits of seeing a doctor rather than how/what it makes you feel. Do not Self-diagnose.

Keep track of your health information and know your family history.

There is no doubt that some people struggle a fair share with others, but it is no excuse not to be on top of your game. When you eventually go to the hospital or clinic, endeavor to answer all the questions the doctor throws at you, in all honesty, no matter how embarrassing it may be to you. Giving the doctor the wrong information can be more dangerous than ever.

Protect your Skin and Stay Hydrated
This has to do with sunscreens and fluid. Wearing sunscreens is an excellent way to protect your skin from the sun's harmful rays. Investing in good sunscreens is a decision you are not going to regret. Applying sunscreens can help you prevent skin cancer and keep you looking healthy. Drinking enough water daily is good for keeping yourself adequately hydrated, digestion, circulation, and skin. The average adult should have at least 8-10 glasses or 2 liters of water daily. Your skin and internal organs will be very grateful for that.

Exercise
Exercising will keep your body, mind, and soul fit. If you are self-conscious, you don't have to have an extravagant routine or even go to the gym. You can start a simple pattern from the comfort of your home each morning until you are ready to go outside.

Taking Charge of your Future/Life

To take charge of your life, knowing who you are and what you want is compulsory. What are your likes and dislikes? What are your strengths and weaknesses? You have to be accountable and show up when you're required to do so. Without these and the likes, you cannot truly take charge of your future and life.

Here are five ways to take charge of your future and life:

Stop The Comparison

Comparison will lead you to unhappiness faster than a jet in the sky, and social media doesn't make it any easier. Every day, we are reminded that our peers are doing much better than us, a recipe for misery and ill health.

You have to focus on your path and not anyone else's. You can turn social media into a platform that inspires you to be the best version of yourself. It is all about perspective, and once you begin to see social media as a tool for achieving your goals rather than a tool for oppression by those who you think are far ahead of you, you are on the right path to take charge.

Be Accountable

A lot of charge-taking involves your ability to be responsible, accountable, and worthy of recommendation. You can't continue to hide behind your fears and excuses because that makes you unreliable and untrustworthy.

Take Your Dreams Seriously

No one will do it for you. Part of taking charge of your life and future is to be intentional about your dreams. Having 20 different objectives and goals in six months speaks volumes about the level of seriousness you have about your life.

Today you want to open a fashion shop. Next week, it's a beauty salon. And the next, a retail shop for make-up products. This is the sign of a person that isn't ready to take charge. Picking a particular goal and standing by it because you believe in it, no matter how long it'll take to actualize, is a deal breaker.
Some of you give up easily. You take two steps back whenever challenges arise because you're scared of confrontation.

It's okay to feel that way, but what's not okay is to remain the same person who is afraid to face challenges, year in and year out.

Believe in your dreams first, and watch people believe in them.

Cultivate an Act of Gratitude
You can cultivate this attitude by taking a daily record of what you are grateful for. Make it a habit so that it will become a part of you. At the same time, I try to find new things to be grateful for each day. If you lay on your couch all day, you can't find those things. Take a walk, explore new places, and try fresh food.

Do something different each day. Be intentional about being grateful.

Taking Charge of Your Happiness
We often look outside of ourselves to find happiness. We try to put our happiness at bay until we meet specific goals. 'I'll be joyful when I get a boyfriend. I'll be happy when I get a new job. I'll be happy when my pay comes

in.' We have conditioned happiness only to come after we hit certain milestones, forgetting that happiness is a choice and doesn't have to go with any criteria.

Ways You Can Take Charge of Your Happiness

There are many ways to take charge of your happiness and revel in it. Find some of them below:

Find Ways to Laugh
It can be difficult to laugh in the face of difficulties. But finding humor is essential if you want to take control of your life; it keeps you going.

As they say, laughter is the most potent medicine. Yes, it is, and the good news is that laughter costs nothing. Laughter is good for your health; indulge it often. Watch a comedy, and hang around people that evoke laughter in you.

Surround Yourself with Positive Energy
This will take us back to energy vampires, and I have already covered that topic in this book. Essentially, what you must not do is surround yourself with energy vampires and anything that will drain you of your energy. The only kind of energy you need around you is positive energy and the ones that will make you feel alive and well.

As you surround yourself with positive energy, also make sure you give positive vibes to the people around you. Remember, what you give comes back to you.

Create and Maintain Relationships
At this point, you already know that your happiness shouldn't be tied to the relationships and friendships that you create, but at the same time, understanding that you cannot survive on your own is paramount.

Having and maintaining relationships creates mental and emotional stimulation, which helps you boost your overall mood.

Be a Forgiver
Keeping grudges will only dampen your spirit and make you bitter. Forgiveness does more for you than the person you're forgiving. It can be difficult to forgive when you consider the gravity of the pain the person has caused, but you're doing it for yourself at the end of the day. You're a forgiver so that you can be free.

Stop Feeling Sorry for Yourself
I used to bask in self-pity when I was much younger. I had the 'poor-me syndrome .' It is when a person labels the world and everyone around them as harsh, cruel, and unfair. In fairness, everything happening around me at that time was enough to make me feel sorry for myself. It got to a time when I began to get angry at others for not feeling sorry for me. I mean, couldn't they see what I was going through? Didn't they see how hard things were for me? And every time a person showed that they felt pity for me, I felt very validated. I felt like I was eventually being seen. It was a depressing time for me. I didn't get better until I became self-positive.

- I do need pity. Pity will not solve my problems.
- No matter how challenging my condition is, it will not crush me.
- I am strong enough to deal with my problems.

The poor-me syndrome is one of the most childish and immature traits anyone can possess. If you think you have this syndrome, you must take measures to curb it because it can hinder your growth and stop you from reaching your peak.

A Little Love Note for You

My dear black woman, I hope you read this love note. So this is a little love note from a sister girl to another sister girl.

I understand that you feel very overwhelmed on some days. Some days, you feel like you're about to be crushed under the weight of your responsibilities. Suppose you're all alone in the world, existing and drained. I feel that way sometimes too. It used to be very frequent when I had poor knowledge of myself. But the more I morph into this powerful woman, the more the feeling disappears.

I'm writing this love note to remind you that we are wholly and deeply loved; no matter what happens, that love will not fade away. It's okay not to be okay every day. What is not okay is allowing the feeling to engulf you and crush you. The bad days come and go. The sun will rise, and you will be happy again.

I love you so much. It is an absolute pleasure and honor to write this book for you. I hope my love for you glows through these pages as you read.

I am your cheerleader, sister. I love you.

Conclusion

Feminine energy is a powerful but not talked about enough energy. That is why I seized the day and wrote a whole book about it for women like me who are curious about all it entails and how to master it and use it to one's advantage.

While writing this book, I knew I needed to make it relatable to everyone who reads it. That's what inspired me to use personal and relatable stories that are relevant to the discourse.

I hope you enjoyed reading till this point. I hope you remember never to neglect your feminine energy too. Please go into the world and conquer it with the magic of your feminine energy. You are all the greatness that you think you are and more.

I love you!

Thank You

You could have picked from dozens of other books, but you picked our bundle of 2 books

Divine Feminine Energy

So, THANK YOU for getting this book and for making it all the way to the end.

Could you please consider posting a review on Amazon or if you get the Audio version then on Audible?

Posting a positive review is the best and easiest way to support the work of independent authors like me.

Your feedback will help me to keep writing the kind of books that will help you get the results you want.

It can be something short and simple ☺

Thank you so much

www.ingramcontent.com/pod-product-compliance
Lightning Source LLC
Chambersburg PA
CBHW072052110526
44590CB00018B/3133